ATTILA THE HUN

LEADERSHIP ▪ STRATEGY ▪ CONFLICT

NIC FIELDS ▪ ILLUSTRATED BY STEVE NOON

First published in Great Britain in 2015 by Osprey Publishing,
PO Box 883, Oxford, OX1 9PL, UK
PO Box 3985, New York, NY 10185-3985, USA
E-mail: info@ospreypublishing.com
© 2015 Osprey Publishing Limited

Osprey Publishing is part of Bloomsbury Ltd.

Print ISBN: 978 1 4728 0887 5
PDF e-book ISBN: 978 14728 0888 2
EPUB e-book ISBN: 978 1 4728 0889 9

Editorial by Ilios Publishing Ltd, Oxford, UK (www.iliospublishing.com)
Cartography: Bounford.com
Index by Angela Hall
Originated by PDQ Media, Bungay, UK
Printed in China through Worldprint Ltd.

15 16 17 18 19   10 9 8 7 6 5 4 3 2 1

A CIP catalogue record for this book is available from the British Library.

The Woodland Trust

Osprey Publishing are supporting the Woodland Trust, the UK's leading
woodland conservation charity, by funding the dedication of trees.
www.ospreypublishing.com

Artist's note

Readers may care to note that the original paintings from which the
colour plates in this book were prepared are available for private sale.
All reproduction copyright whatsoever is retained by the Publishers. All
enquiries should be addressed to:

www.steve-noon.co.uk

The Publishers regret that they can enter into no correspondence upon
this matter.

Contents

INTRODUCTION

We all struggle to leave markers behind, signs that we were here, that we passed through. Yet for the fortunate few there is the imperishable remembrance as 'the Great', 'the Calligrapher', 'the Conqueror', 'the Pious', 'the Navigator', 'the Magnificent', and so on. Characters venerated in history, their names have resounded down the ages. Not forgetting of course the celebrated arch-villains of history, 'the Cruel', 'the Lame', 'the Impaler', 'the Terrible', 'the Ripper', 'the Butcher', and so on. And then there was the king of the Huns, Attila, who seemingly styled himself *flagellum Dei*, 'the Scourge of God'. It has a certain ring, you must agree.

The name Attila is in all likelihood derived from *ata*, 'father' in modern Turkish, and by means of the diminutive *-ila* we can arrive at 'Little Father'. If this is correct, then it may not even have been his original name at all, but a term of affection and respect conferred on his accession, a Hun version of *Atatürk* ('Father of the Turkish Nation') by which Mustafa Kemal Paşa was known. If the man we call Attila had a personal name, it has long been lost.

Be that as it may, under Attila's rule the Hun Empire occupied an impressive area. With its heartland fixed firmly on the Hungarian steppe, the *puszta*, in the north Attila's domain extended to what was then known as the Mare Suevicum (Baltic Sea), where, according to Priscus, a Greek-speaking Roman historian, an eyewitness and our most important source for the life of Attila, 'he ruled even the islands of the Ocean' (fr. 8). It did not quite stretch to the Rhenus (Rhine), for the Franks and the Burgundians lay in between, but he was said by Priscus to rule 'all Scythia' (fr. 8), that is, all the lands west of the

Relief in the form of a medallion (*c.*1550) from La Certosa di Pavia monastery showing a demonic portrait of Attila by Giovanni Antonio Amadeo. It bears the evocative inscription ATILA FLAGELVM DEI. (akg-images)

Mare Caspium (Caspian Sea). Whether Attila was a great empire builder is a moot point. Jordanes (d. AD 583) had no doubt. 'Attila', the Romanized Goth wrote, 'was lord over all the Huns and almost the sole earthly ruler of all the tribes of Scythia, a man marvellous for his glorious fame among all nations' (*Get.* 178, cf. 181). Modern commentators tend to be more sceptical. Attila delighted in war, and initially his power sprang from bowstrings and hooves. However, after he had ascended the throne, his head, rather than his arm, had achieved the conquests towards the north. During this period the East Roman Empire had successfully bought off its formidable new neighbours, but now injudiciously allowed its payments of tribute to fall in arrears.

Until the end of the AD 430s the Huns were an almighty annoyance, much worse than the wild Saracens or the Isaurian bandits, but they were not a peril. Their inroads carried them deep into the Balkan provinces, but they were always either driven out or bought off. At the end of the following decade, the Huns were, in the words of a defrocked patriarch of Constantinople, 'the masters, and the Romans the slaves' (Nestorius, 368). An exaggeration, but no courtier in Constantinople could have denied that within a few years a barbarian band of robbers had grown into a major military power. The change was the ascendancy of Attila. A new phase now began.

By now Europe has happily forgotten the terror of Attila and his Huns – just one of those phases of disruption and anarchy that is the opportunity of the military adventurer from the oceanic vastness of the Eurasian steppes – and nowadays horse nomads are picturesque, palling cultures to be preserved and patronized. Back then, however, the Huns terrified people by their outlandish appearance, and their very name soon became the epitome of swift, merciless destruction. Branded by the philosopher and theologian Isidorus Hispalensis (d. AD 636) as the 'rod of divine anger' (*virga furoris dei sunt*, *HV* 29, cf. Isaiah 14:5), the Huns had become a faceless horde, terrible and subhuman, 'fiercer than ferocity itself' (AM 31.2.21).

This Hun skull (Wien, Kunsthistorisches Museum) has been deliberately constricted with fabric bandages so that it grew excessively tall and conical. Archaeology tells us that the Huns bound the heads of some of their children, both male and female, who retained their deformed skulls as adults. Yet, oddly enough, no late antique source records seeing any such thing. As Mann suggests, maybe 'the long-heads were an elite' (2005: 66). If so, did Attila have a skull that was artificially deformed? (Ancient Art & Architecture)

Out of Asia

Originating from the Inner Asian steppe, the Huns were horse nomads, probably of Turkic stock and speaking a proto-Turkic language. They were possibly the remnants of migrating Xiongnu, a steppe people discussed at some length below, and were certainly nothing to do with the Germanic tribes into whom they so rudely barged. As hunters and herdsmen, they employed the horse and the bow for warlike as well as peaceful purposes, a topic that will prove important below. Steppe nomads had always been a threat to the settled agrarian societies, and beyond the 4th-century Roman frontiers the major event was the arrival of the Huns, who had spread westward across the vast

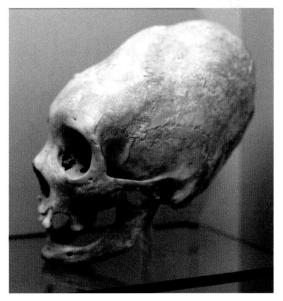

Loup sauve Troyes d'Attila, stained-glass window, Église Saint-Pierre-et-Saint-Paul, Épernay. According to St Lupus of Troyes (AD 383–478/9), when asked who he was, Attila came back with a smart *bon mot*, in impeccable classical Latin of course, '*Ego sum Attila, flagellum Deï*'. (G. Garitan)

billiard table known as the Eurasian steppes from their original homeland on the western slopes of the Altai. Their outriders reached the Jaxartes (Syr Darya) by the AD 340s, the Rha (Volga) by the following decade, and it was around the AD 370s, a generation before the birth of Attila, that they began to migrate even further westward, launching a series of attacks upon the Germanic Goths, who in turn crossed to the right bank of the Danubius (Danube) and desperately sought asylum in Thrace.

It was inevitable that the Huns themselves would sooner or later cross the Danubius into Thrace. The death of the fanatic Christian Theodosius I in January AD 395, the subsequent split of the Roman Empire between his two feeble sons, Arcadius (aged 18, ruler of the East) and Honorius (aged 11, ruler of the West), and the activities of Alaric and Stilicho – Jerome's 'half-barbarian traitor' (*Ep.* 123.17) – in the west meant there was little to stop the Huns in the east. When the Danubius froze in the harsh winter of that year, the Huns rode into Roman territory.

As for their origin, this is, in truth, a mystery. For Ammianus Marcellinus it was not a matter for speculation as the Huns were 'a race of men … which had risen from some secret corner of the earth' (AM 27.5.8). Modern scholarship has thought otherwise, and one theory about the Huns is their possible identification with the warlike people known as the Xiongnu (Pinyin: *Xiōngnú*), a confederation of steppe tribes, probably of Turkic stock, who harassed the Chinese at the end of the Warring States period (475–221 BC) and into the Han dynasty (206 BC – AD 220). Their heyday was under Modu Chanyu (Pinyin: *Mòdú Chányú*), a singularly ruthless proto-Attila, whose spectacular rise is recorded by Sima Qian (b. *c.*140 BC), China's earliest chronicler. Modu Chanyu became *shan-yü* or khan of his people by murdering his father, and his subsequent 35-year rule (209–174 BC) saw the Xiongnu rise to unity and then to empire (Sima Qian *Shiji* 1.110). But their steppe empire went the way of all empires, and the Xiongnu were eventually thrown back by the Chinese into the void of Inner Asia to become rootless horse nomads once again. The major stretch of the Great Wall, in its various manifestations, was constructed on the Xiongnu frontier, and in the words of Sima Qian, 'inside are those who don the cap and girdle, outside are the barbarians' (*Shiji* 38). The Xiongnu were literally 'beyond the pale', the wrong side of civilization's rampart.

The coming of the Huns

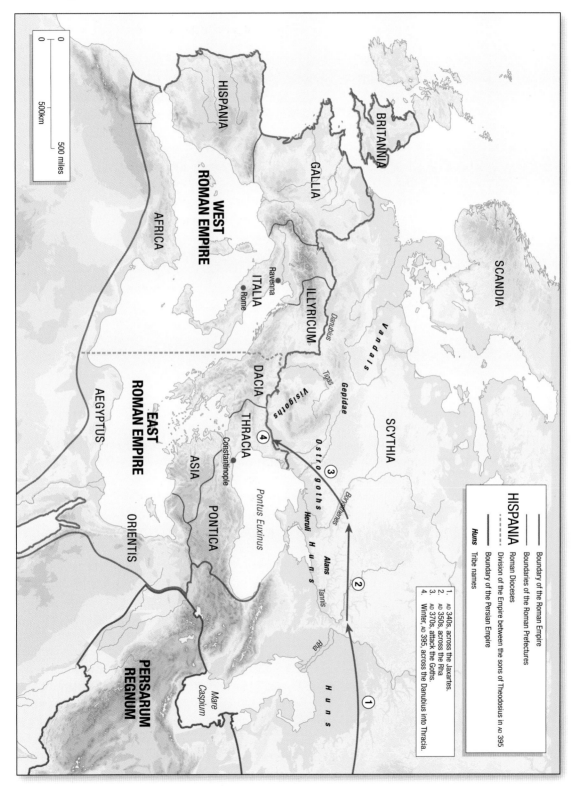

Legend:

HISPANIA   Boundary of the Roman Empire
Boundaries of the Roman Prefectures
Roman Dioceses
Division of the Empire between the sons of Theodosius in AD 395
Boundary of the Persian Empire

Huns   Tribe names

1. AD 340s, across the Jaxartes.
2. AD 350s, across the Rha.
3. AD 370s, attack the Goths.
4. Winter, AD 395, across the Danubius into Thracia.

7

As well as mentally marking a line between 'them' and 'us', the very act of drawing a boundary is an acknowledgement that the peoples excluded are not under control and cannot be ruled by command. They must be dealt with by negotiation. The negotiation that works best is one of enlisting the services of the very tribes that are supposedly excluded by the boundary, thus turning them about so that they face away from the boundary instead of toward it, the time-honoured tradition of 'using barbarian against barbarian', or divide and rule. This can be seen in the Chinese, Roman and British-Indian empires alike.

Yet a more effective form of resistance to China's northern barbarians may have been the adoption of some of their weird methods of mobile warfare. Against the vehement protests of his nobles, Wuling of Zhao (r. 325–298 BC) began 'to wear the costumes of the barbarians' – presumably the close-fitting tunic and kaftan and soft leather boots and trousers, apparel better suited to horseback – and trained his soldiers in mounted archery, who were also given a large meat ration (Sima Qian *Shiji* 110). Presumably the high-protein diet was to make Wuling's men more aggressive as well as beef them up. Anyway, when Wuling took the offensive he employed the tactics of nomad warfare – swift movement in open terrain, appearing and disappearing, laying ambushes and traps, and sudden strikes from nowhere, what we would nowadays recognize as flexible, hard-to-target, guerrilla warfare tactics – and thus broke the hold of the steppe tribes along his kingdom's northern border. Though cavalry was used by all the feudal states during the age of the Warring States, this was China's first body of horse archers (Selby 2003: 174). As the wise Wuling obviously appreciated, whereas campaigning in China demanded only that an army be not too cumbrous to make long marches yet strong enough to overawe the opposition, war in the steppes required technical virtuosity.

Certainly the Xiongnu's devastating technique of warfare, terrifying to the Chinese, was precisely that used with such effect by the Huns some five centuries later against the equally civilized Romans – brilliant riding skills, combined with the dexterous use of a composite bow short enough to fire in any direction from horseback, even straight backwards over the animal's rump, the deservedly famous 'Parthian shot' (distorting in English into 'parting shot') depicted in Han dynasty art. The Han emperors attempted to buy peace from their bothersome neighbours with massive gifts of silk, wine, grain and other foodstuffs, and even on one occasion with the hand in marriage of a princess from the imperial household (Sima Qian *Shiji* 110). Frequent gifts of the embellishments of civilized life, coupled with music and women,

Feast of Attila (1870), fresco (Budapest, Hungarian National Gallery), by the Hungarian artist Mór Than (1828–99) and based on Priscus fr. 8. Attila is in the centre, the young man is his eldest son Ellac, while the two women at top right and left are two of his wives, one of which would be his principal wife, the Germanic princess Herekan. Priscus himself is on the right holding the book labelled ΙΣΤΩΡΙΑ (an incorrect spelling of the Greek ΙΣΤΟΡΙΑ, history). The gentleman in the antiquated corselet and seated to his left is the chief Roman ambassador Maximinus, one of the abler civil servants and diplomats of his day. (Hungarian National Gallery)

it was felt, would distract and enervate even these most warlike people. Nonetheless, too little is known about Hun origins to identify them positively with the Xiongnu, but the latter were decidedly Hun-like and it is sorely tempting to see the Huns of Roman history as the Xiongnu of Chinese history, reborn in poverty.

All that said, tribes fought other tribes on the steppes, and the seeds of the Hun movement westward may lay in desperation. The steppe tribes oscillated between a peaceful and a predatory existence. They would keep to their ancestral grasslands while the going was good, but were quite prepared to invade the grazing lands of others and repel invasions of their own lands when severe weather conditions drove the horse nomads and their controlled herds here and there over the Inner Asian steppe (more properly, steppe nomads were pastoral peoples, for they did not normally migrate voluntarily over vast distances). Thus, it may have been a series of particularly devastating droughts – a regular hazard on the semi-arid steppes where rainfall is limited to 250–500ml a year – which broke the usual grazing cycles of horse nomads around the Aral and Caspian seas and spurred the Huns on to new pastures, and thus clashes with the Alans and the Goths.

Yet climate alone is not a sufficient explanation, for to a lesser tribe drought would have proved fatal. It is therefore at least a reasonable conjecture that the Huns were a confederation of pastoral tribes that moved westward. The nomadic way of life and the common hardships that such a lifestyle presented resulted in a degree of cultural unity among all the steppe dwellers of Inner Asia. With the right mixture of need, self-interest and leadership, these ethnic nomad groupings could come together to forge alliances, and then would fall apart to fight among themselves with great speed. The pastoral peoples had a legend in which a mother figure rebuked her quarrelling sons by telling them each to take an arrow and break it – something they could do easily. Then she told them to put together as many arrows as there were sons and break them – something none of them could do (Selby 2003: 260). Unity in strength. As we shall find out in due course, Attila and his sons failed to remember such folkloric wisdom.

Then again this Hun movement may have been the result of a pressure of population. As it happens, the 4th century and the early 5th century AD in northern China were tumultuous, a 'dark age' between the great days of Han and Tang, sometimes referred to as the Period of Disunion. The chaos lessened somewhat when a Turkic group, the Toba, established north of the Yangtze a sinicized dynasty known as the Northern Wei (Pinyin: *Běi Wěi*) in AD 386. Yet the emergence and collapse of Chinese dynasties may have sent shock waves of refugees westward.

Imitative gold medallion depicting Valens (Wien, Kunsthistorisches Museum, inv. 32.481), from the Szilágysomlyó treasure, discovered in 1797 and 1889 in two locations in the village of Szilágysomlyó, now known as Şimleu Silvaniei, Transylvania. The legend reads: D(omi)N(vs) VALENS P(ivs) F(elix) AVG(vstvs). It is the work of a skilled Gothic craftsman. (Standstein)

The Eurasian steppes, which span Eurasia for over 6,000km from Manchuria in north-eastern Chine to Hungary in eastern Europe and are bounded by the Taiga forests in the north and a desert belt to the south, have long been an open highway between Inner Asia and Europe. Before the Huns came the Sauromatians and Sarmatians, as would the Avars, Magyars, Pechenegs and Cumans after them. Yet these migrations rarely involved hordes of whip-snapping horsemen thundering at full gallop across the treeless, rolling steppes. The metaphors 'waves', 'tides' and 'hordes' are misleading and obscure the fact that the movement of peoples toward the west was a gradual process that extended over many centuries. For some groups, it took generations to move the few hundred kilometres from the Volga to the Dnieper, still longer to make it to the Danube. After all, those who arrived from the east were horse nomads, and with rare exceptions they deliberately moved slowly, always conscious of the need for adequate grazing lands and water for their mixed herds.

We must not therefore picture the Huns as pouring in from the vast steppes of Eurasia in one enormous multitude. In ecological terms that would have been unsustainable. Simply by looking at their methods of producing and appropriating food it is evident that a very large area of grazing land and hunting ground was necessary to support a comparatively small number of Huns, the primary unit of Hun society being the extended family. Comparisons with modern horse nomads in Inner Asia, where the family group is still the central structure in their lives, suggest that clans of between 500 and 1,000 members make good economic sense. There were no Hun 'hordes'.

Likewise, we must not push the Huns way down the ladder of societal evolution. As they did not till the soil, Huns derived the bulk of their food from their herds – horses, cattle, goats, and, above all, sheep, but not pigs – and, much like other steppe dwellers, they had to augment their supply by foraging, fishing and hunting (AM 31.2.3, Claud. *In Ruf.* 1.327, Prisc. *apud* Jord. *Get.* 123, cf. 37). Additionally, Huns obtained their grain through barter or as tribute from their settled neighbours on the steppe-rim. According to anthropological field studies conducted by ethnographers working among the horse nomads of what was then Soviet Asia, a nomadic family of four required up to 260kg of meat per year, 8–10 litres of milk or milk products every day, and 2–3kg of grain or substitute. So every year 15–17 sheep (or 20–25 goats, or two to three bull-calves) had to be slaughtered for meat, and four to five

Pair of woman's *fibulae* (Wien, Kunsthistorisches Museum, inv. U1, U2), gold foil on silver with inlaid garnet, glass and enamel, *c.* AD 430. These were part of the Untersiebenbrunn treasure discovered in 1910 in the town of Untersiebenbrunn, Lower Austria, in a 5th-century grave belonging to an either Gepidic or Alanic princess. The Gepids (*Gepidae*) were a Germanic people closely related to the Goths, the Alans (*Alani*) originally a Transcaucasan nomadic people. (James Steakley)

milch cows or not less than 15 goats had to be kept (Vainshtein 1980: 104). To these we must add a string of horses for riding and a couple of oxen for haulage. Within its norm the steppe life produced the essentials of food – and of course clothing (hides), housing (felts) and fuel (dung). Pastoralists may have more than enough for the necessities of life, but they always lack what we would recognize as comforts and luxuries. Under strict steppe conditions accessories threaten mobility, and thus survival. Life on these terms is a life without trimmings. A true nomad is a poor nomad. Yet to have a more convenient existence, nomads depend on their sedentary neighbours, either through trade, diplomacy, raids or conquest.

The steppe in Mongolia. The harsh environment of the steppe was where the Huns fostered the skills of formidable fighters. (InvictaHOG)

So the Huns were poorer, less coordinated, and less heavily armed than farm-minded soldiers, but they were enormously mobile, being mounted on horses. Moreover, they could put practically their entire male population of military age into battle. The military system was simple: everyone between the ages of 15 and 50 was a horse warrior, tending their herds and hunting when at peace and forming a war band in times of war. On a plundering expedition a raiding force probably numbered about 1,000 horse warriors at the most, with some old men left behind to look after, alongside the women and the children, the herds. With the menfolk out raiding, the herds may have been left in the capable hands of the women and children, but women would ride on horseback as much and as well as men, while their children, boys and girls alike, were taught to ride horses, with and without saddles, from an early age. In the time of Procopius of Caesarea (b. *c.*AD 500), when the Huns had reverted to a form of social organization similar to

A Turkic felt tent (*yurt* or *ger*) with a collapsible frame, a latticework made of poplar and willow. Erected, the whole structure would be secured by stout pegged ropes. The black felt covering was proof against wind and rain, thereby providing good insulation and protection from severe steppe weather. (© Nic Fields)

that in which they were living before the rule of Attila, their forces nearly always appear to number between 200 and 1,200 men, and he clearly says (*Wars* 8.3.10) that women were found fighting in their ranks. The expedition of Zabergan in AD 558, which aroused so much terror in Constantinople and was composed of 7,000 Kotrigur Huns, was a noted exception (Agath. 5.22).

By comparison, sedentary people greatly outnumbered pastoral people because farming feeds far more mouths from the same area of land

than herding. However, a nomadic society that can put all of its men into highly mobile raiding parties can take on an agrarian society of ten times its population with a good prospect of success. If the extreme of wealth was the patch of intensively cultivated land in a well-watered valley, the extreme of mobility was the mounted warrior out of the steppe. It was this combination of mobility and economic independence that made the Huns so formidable in war, in spite of their conspicuously small numbers. Yet the mounted nomad warrior lost mobility in proportion as he accumulated the loot of settled civilization, and in doing so he lost the very factor that had given him mastery.

Into Europe

'No human community is, or ever has been, entirely static: the society of the Huns was more dynamic than most.' So wrote the eminent Marxist historian of the 'barbarians' of this period, E. A. Thompson (1948: 3). Political events are only the surface phenomena of history. The forces that create them lie deeper, and these forces derive from the interaction of society and environment. When this is borne in mind, the popular image of Huns rampaging across Roman Europe seems to be highly misleading. It is often said the Huns were rough, uncultured herdsmen, but they had been rubbing shoulders with agrarian societies for centuries, and had learned to value the qualities of these people and their culture while maintaining their own self-esteem and cultural heritage. It is more correct to say that by the time of Attila's birth the Huns had adopted many cultural characteristics from those Germanic peoples whom they had conquered, and from non-Turkic steppe nomads such as the Iranian Alans, a subgroup of the Sarmatians who had previously dominated the western steppes.

The Huns also became accustomed to wealth acquired through booty and tribute from the Roman Empire, which allowed them to buy the advantages of agrarian civilization too. Put simply, the relatively gentler life on the *puszta* had changed their nature.

These European Huns, as opposed to those who had remained on the Inner Asian steppe, lived a rapacious rather than a nomadic way of life, and therefore should not be seen as a purely pastoral society. One of our most important eyewitnesses, Priscus of Panium, found Attila living in a 'very large village' (fr. 8) where the nobility had enclosures with adorned palisades of smooth square timber, studded with towers, but intended rather for decoration than defence. There was even a fully functional Roman-style bathhouse made of imported stone. This was not the steppe. The keen, critical, analytical powers of Gibbon concluded very plausibly that the origin of Attila's seat of empire 'could be no more than an accidental camp, which, by long and frequent residence of Attila, had insensibly swelled into a huge village' (*D&F*, chap. XXXV, p. 386). Clearly, in unifying the European Huns under his autocratic rule, Attila had established for himself a permanent capital.

Hunnic cauldron (Budapest, Magyar Nemzeti Múzeum), 4th century AD. One of the signature artefacts brought by the Huns to central Europe was the thick bronze cauldron common to the horse nomads in Inner Asia. This huge, cumbersome, bell-shaped cooking-pot with hefty handles, often ending in flat mushroom-shaped lugs, was big enough to boil up clan-size stews. Broiled or stewed was thus the manner Huns preferred their meat, not half-raw. (© Bridgeman Art Library)

The available archaeological evidence from the middle and lower Danube region does not show a dramatic socioeconomic change with the arrival of the Huns. It looks as if Hun villages, which were fixed settlements dominated by surface dwellings with wattle-and-daub walls, clay-coated floors and reed-thatched roofs, were plentiful on the *puszta*, and were well supplied with the fruits of agriculture, viz. millet, rye and barley (Elton 1997: 28–29). It is important to remember that the *puszta*, the largest area of steppe land within central Europe, was very small compared to the Eurasian steppes to the east. In other words, it was not extensive enough to sustain the perennial nomadic way of life the Huns had followed on the Inner Asian steppe. Moreover, it was also crisscrossed by rivers and streams and marked by marshes and forests, which would make the maintenance of a nomadic horse army very difficult. It has been estimated by one modern scholar that the pasturage of the *puszta* could only support some 150,000 grazing nomad horses. By analogy with the later Mongols, it is considered that each Hun required a herd of ten horses – on campaign a warrior took not one horse but a string of them, affording him fresh, quick mounts on demand – and thus there were only 15,000 Hun horse warriors in this period (Lindner 1981: 14–15).

Even if Lindner's estimates for the grazing potential of the *puszta* are taken as gospel, this interpretation should not mean the European Huns had turned soft and urbanized and given up their horses, let alone stopped practising their ancestral accomplishments of the equestrian arts and archery skills. After all, mounted archery was not only their heritage, but their astonishing success came from the union of horse and bow too. Thus it can be said that although they now lived in permanent villages on the *puszta*, the unmistakable mounted warfare of steppe nomadism did not disappear with the autocratic Attila, a king who certainly ruled his empire without leaving the back of his horse. What we should imagine, therefore, is an empire in which a nomadic minority, backed by a reliably strong albeit relatively small nomadic horse army, rule an extremely heterogeneous, multiethnic and mixed nomadic-sedentary population. We have a suitable and contemporary parallel with the Toba horse warriors, offshoots of the same old central Asian tree as the Huns, with whom they shared a cultural archery heritage. Like many successful conquest dynasties in China, the Northern Wei dynasty (AD 386–534) straddled the steppe and the sown, combining the military effectiveness of a nomadic horse army with a willingness to rule their Chinese sedentary territories so as to maximize the productiveness of the agricultural sector.

Przewalski's horse *(equus ferus Przewalskii)*, Khustain Nuruu National Park, Mongolia, the ancestor of some breeds in Inner Asia and China. Common to the Eurasian steppes, Hun horses were tough, rough-coated mounts with short legs. Though only 12–14 hands, they were muscular and had great stamina, their smallness affording the Huns considerable control over them, qualities not lost on the Romans, even if the horses were contemptuously referred to as 'hardy but ugly beasts' (AM 31.2.5). In his classification of various breeds according to their fitness for war, Vegetius (*Mul.* 3.6.2) gives the Hun horse the first place because of its patience, perseverance, and its capacity to endure cold and hunger. (Chinneeb)

THE EARLY YEARS

The nomadic lifestyle favoured those with physical prowess, who were quick with the bow, capable of outwitting the wiles of the hunted. And it was the hunt that served to hone military skills during peacetime when they were not needed to defend or expand the grazing territory. In his account of the Xiongnu, Sima Qian describes how the new Han dynasty found itself faced with an old menace on its northern borders, that is, steppe tribes skilled in mounted archery:

> The Xiongnu had no written language: they govern themselves on the basis of the spoken word alone. Infants could ride a goat and draw a bow to shoot small birds and rats. As they grew up, they would shoot foxes and hares and these are what they used to eat. Their warriors were powerful archers, and all were armoured horsemen. Their custom when at peace was to follow their flocks, and thus archery and hunting formed part of their way of life. When war threatened, they practised battles and attacks so that they could invade or make unexpected attacks. This was part of their very nature. (Sima Qian *Shiji* 58)

Whether in the chase or on the battlefield, the bow represented the greatest empowerment of the individual, young and old alike, over his environment. This was the way of all steppe tribes.

As a youth, therefore, the Hun's challenge was to master the use of the horse and bow in battle and to persuade his elders by his courage in facing the wolf in the hunt so that he might, in time, make a worthy horse warrior of a horse warrior people. The Hun grew up in a society where there were no civilians. To be a poor fighter and hunter was to fail as a man and as a free Hun. As a later Khitan proverb explains, 'Our wealth is in our horses and our strength is in our warriors. Drawing a strong bow to kill game provides us with our daily needs' (cited in Selby 2003: 232). The Khitan (Pinyin: *Qìdān*) were a nomadic Mongolic people who established the Liao dynasty of China (AD 907–1125).

A condensed account of the Huns themselves would seem not to be out of place at this point. As just alluded to, their pre-eminence as warriors derived primarily from their mastery of the

Terracotta *haniwa* horse (Edinburgh, Royal Museum, inv. 10.73-6) from Osato district, Saitama province, Japan, 7th century AD. It carries the universal wood-framed saddle of the Asiatic horse archer, its high front and back arches providing plenty of support and a secure seat for the archer to discharge his arrows in any direction. Huns used one of a similar design, usually of birch wood. Into the wood they rubbed sheep fat in order to protect it from water damage. The incised line terminating in a loop represents a mounting stirrup. Attached to only one side of the saddle, this provided the rider with an easier and safer method of mounting his horse, nothing more. (© Nic Fields)

horse, secondly from their skill as archers. Late antique authors such as Ammianus Marcellinus (31.2.6), Jerome (*Ep*. 60.7), Justin (41.3.4) and Zosimus (4.20.4) describe them eating, sleeping, and even performing bodily functions from horseback, pardonable exaggerations. For though their horses' backs were not their only abode, in their day the Huns were incomparable horsemen, riding the ill-shaped but hardy steppe breed of horse, though it must be said that contact with the Roman world meant they later acquired stall-fed Roman chargers too (Oros. 7.34.5). Stall-fed horses, which have their hay and grain brought to them, can do more work than pasture-fed horses, which therefore allowed the individual Hun to maintain a smaller herd of horses as campaign-ready remounts.

So mounted, the swift-riding Hun fought with small shield and spear, and, above all, a composite recurve bow with which he was highly skilled even when drawn from a galloping or wheeling horse. The stave of the composite recurve bow was constructed of laminated materials, usually wood (core), sinew (back), and horn (belly), with seven bone plates stiffening both the grip and the extremities or 'ears', three on the grip and a pair on each ear. The bow was held together with a natural, water-soluble fish or bone glue and then waterproofed by lacquering. When strung, the bow was opened back against its natural curve and held that way by the bowstring, whence the term recurve. This meant that greater latent power could be stored in the bow than could be stored by bending a straight stick. More powerful even than the famed English longbow (and even many types

of bullet), a well-made composite recurve bow could shoot an arrow through an iron breastplate or 15mm of wood at close range, say 50–100m. The art of shooting from horseback was clearly an advance over merely carrying the bow while riding, and the deadeye accuracy with which the Hun used this peculiarly powerful weapon never failed to astound the late antique authors (AM 31.2.9, Olymp. fr. 18, SA *Carm.* 2.266–69, Jord. *Get.* 249, *Wars* 1.27.27, 6.1.9–10).

According to Ammianus Marcellinus, it worked like this.

A Hunnic army formed up for battle, with much disorderly movement and savage noise, in wedge-shaped masses. Some of these would break up into scattered bands, which would rush around with surprising speed and apparent chaos, inflicting casualties with their shooting. Other bands would relieve the first to maintain an incessant barrage until the enemy was sufficiently weakened or demoralized. Each warrior would then

Horse trappings (Baltimore, Walters Art Museum, inv. 57.1050-2, 1060), gilt bronze and gemstones, 4th century AD. At the top is a chamfron, followed by two bridle mounts and finally a whip handle. What Turkic horsemen call a *kamçi*, the open end would have held the rawhide thongs of the whip, which would have been secured in place by a bronze rivet. Although a Hun carried a whip – this auriferous model being a rather exotic example – it was generally for show or use on dogs, not his precious horse, and certainly no Hun needed spurs to urge his horse to run. (Walters Art Museum)

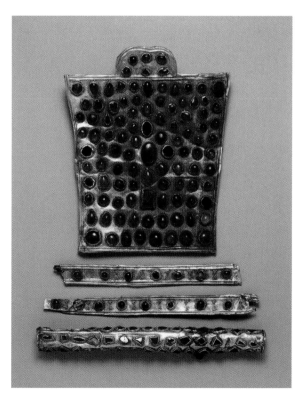

charge at the gallop, he and his horse moving as one and regardless of risk to his own safety, to fight at close-quarters with spear and sword. The plan was simple: a Hun charge was executed with such speed and suddenness that it usually overwhelmed everyone and everything in its path. The Huns relied heavily on mounted archery skills, but they were also skilled in the use of spears and swords. Thus, in the context of a pitched battle, it would be misleading to assume that the Huns were archers alone.

And then there was the lasso. This was not only a common tool of the mounted herder but a natural weapon too, being employed to bring down an enemy horseman or capture someone on foot (AM 31.2.9, Olymp. fr. 18, Mal. 364), the most celebrated example surely being Theotimus, bishop of Tomis, miraculously warding off a Hun's attempt to rope him in (Soz. 7.26.8). Pausanias describes how a lasso was thrown around an enemy and the horse then wheeled away, causing the enemy 'to trip in the tangle of rope' (1.21.8). It was not very sportsmanlike, but it was business. Usually lassoes were made of soft strips of cloth plaited into nooses (AM 31.2.9), and the rider would carry his lasso coiled up and strapped to the rear arch of the saddle, or else slung over his shoulder.

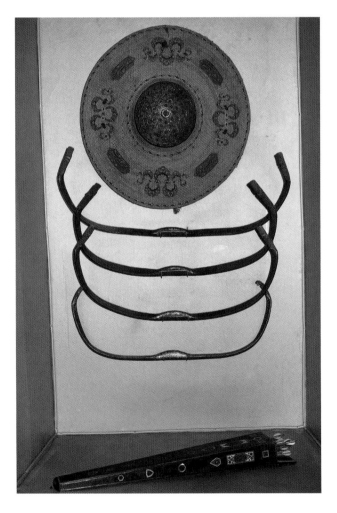

Turkish composite recurve bows and shield, dated 1530/50. The Huns used a composite recurve bow measuring 140–160cm from tip to tip. A man fashioned his own arrows, however, their length equalling the length of his arm to the fingertips. Arrows were kept in an hourglass quiver with a closing flap (seen here, bottom). The shape allowed the accommodation of arrows with barbs up for easier arrowhead selection. (akg-images)

But how does all this relate to the early years of Attila? This is the question we must next address.

The truth is that it is virtually impossible to describe in detail the early years of Attila, nothing being known. He was probably born at the turn of the 5th century AD somewhere on the *puszta*, and his father was called Mundiuch, a brother to Ruga. Suffice it to say that nomadic life required every man – and woman – to ride and shoot from an early age, to develop survival skills and resilience and to adapt to changing circumstances – everything with which this discussion began. And there were daily tasks, such as supervising the herds or participating in hunting, which served as military training too, for both individuals and groups. Indeed, riding would have been the first skill they mastered. Today, Mongol and Kazakh nomads still train both girls and boys to be accomplished riders. Learning to ride almost as soon as they can walk, all children achieve proficiency by the time they are three or so.

What is certain is that from boyhood Attila would have tended horses and grown up skilled in archery from horseback, and perhaps knew the Gothic language too. Under his uncle Ruga, the man whom, it seems, gave the Hun kingdom a firm foundation, Attila would have certainly learnt how to fight the Romans and become familiar with the technique of leading opportunistic raids into their territory. On the other hand, though it is somewhat risky to extrapolate the steppe nomadic ways of the past from present customs, young boys were probably expected to help their mothers too, preparing food, carrying water, milking the livestock, and performing other domestic duties, while girls learned how to ride, shoot and round up herds. The hand that rocked the cradle also could pull a bow.

Attila would have been married at an early age. Steppe tribes were usually exogamous, meaning they married outside the tribe, and marriage alliances were an important device for cementing inter-tribal coalitions. Polygamy was common amongst elites, though there was a distinction between the principal wife and lesser women, and only the sons of the former were eligible as successors for their father's position. Women played an important role in all aspects of tribal life, including fighting of course, and sometimes enjoyed political power. One of the wives of the dead Bleda, Attila's elder brother, ruled over a village. This was the famous occasion when Priscus and his Roman companions were sent 'provisions and good-looking women to comfort them' (Prisc. fr. 8). The latter was a courtesy normally only extended to the highest-ranking Huns. The Romans politely declined, though with what reluctance Priscus does not give away.

Attila had several wives, who presumably bore him several sons and daughters. Attila's principal wife was the Germanic princess Herekan, who gave him three sons, Ellac, Dengizich and Ernach. Priscus knew by sight two of the three sons, having seen the eldest and the youngest at their father's banquet. He even had the honour of meeting their mother. After an exchange of gifts, Herekan briefly interviewed Priscus in her own dwelling. He found the first lady reclining on kilims, wool woven rugs, surrounded by her handmaidens, who were busy embroidering fine linens for the menfolk (Prisc. fr. 8).

On the unexpected death of their uncle Ruga in AD 434, Attila initially ruled with his elder brother Bleda. Although the two brothers always acted in concert, as far as we know, and regarded their empire as a single entity, they divided it between them and ruled separately (Jord. *Get.* 181, *Chron. Min.* 1.4801353, cf. Prisc. fr. 1). According to Maenchen-Helfen, 'Bleda ruled over the tribes in the east, Attila over those in the west' (1973: 86).

In AD 444 or 445 Bleda died. No contemporary evidence exists to support the later allegations that Attila had him murdered (Jord. *Get.* 181, *Chron. Min.* 1.4801555, CM *ad annum* 445). Still, the brothers were quite dissimilar in temperament and had always detested each other. There is a proverb that says the sky cannot have two suns. A man of superior energy must keep a man of lesser energy but comparable ambition in his place or remove

Mughal thumb ring (London, Victoria & Albert Museum, inv. IS 02521) made of white nephrite jade set with emeralds, rubies and a diamond. This was for decorative purpose only. Serious archers, like the Huns who placed a special emphasis and value on archery, preferred thumb rings made of leather, horn or bone, few of which have survived. The thumb-draw is a faster draw, allowing greater speed of delivery than the various types of finger draw, and it also helps prevent the bowstring cutting into the fingers or bruising the forearm of the bow-arm, which can disrupt the aim. Moreover, it is physically more awkward to draw back a bowstring beyond the centre of the body with the fingers hooked over the string, whereas with a thumb ring it becomes easier. But the method is far more difficult to master, proficiency requiring endless practice. (va_va_val)

him altogether. Attila, however nefarious, had the attributes of greatness, whereas Bleda's principal occupation, or so says Priscus, was laughing at his court buffoon, a grotesque Moorish dwarf named Zerko. Before his capture by the Huns Zerko had belonged to the *magister utriusque militiae* Aspar, of whom I will speak at length later on. Attila was clearly not amused by this quirky stand-up comic, and, once Bleda was dead, presented him to Aëtius, who in turn gave him back to Aspar. Bleda had provided Zerko with a Hun wife, and when he wanted to have her sent to him Attila refused (Prisc. fr. 11).

The brothers were members of a tribal dynasty that had slowly gathered Hun clans and tribes under its rule and protection, together with many conquered (and submitted) subject peoples (the majority Germanic) who were engaged in agriculture, trade and handicrafts, to create a substantial empire in eastern and central Europe north of the Danubius. As was discussed above, Hun society was now much more sedentary, having established a capital near the middle reaches of the river Priscus (frs. 8, 9) names Tigas, in all probability the Tisza/Theiss (Hungarian/German), which meanders across the *puszta*, cutting it in two. What is certain is that after Bleda's death there was no suggestion of dual or divided rulership. Attila was acknowledged as the sole ruler of the Huns. He was the first Hun who could make that claim with absolute assurance. He was also to be the last.

THE MILITARY LIFE

Whereas irrigated agriculture makes possible the maximum of intensive economy (viz. heavier crop per acre), pastoral steppe nomadism is notably an extensive economy (viz. dispersal of herds). This in turn makes the population denser in irrigated areas than on the steppes where pastoral nomadism prevails. Yet, the horse gives the nomad speed, range and mobility. So despite a wide dispersal of his society, the mobility of the whole population and its property make it possible for nomad people to get away from military expeditions invading the wide steppe from the settled land. These punitory forces, with their plodding infantry and stall-fed cavalry, are lumbering, logistic-bound leviathans, while the extraordinary galloping mobility of nomad warriors makes them formidable in raiding settled populations. After all, their granaries are worth plundering and their irrigation works not only immobile but vulnerable.

Thus, to obtain what they needed to ease and enliven nomadic life it was common for steppe dwellers to resort to raiding their settled neighbours. Just as Sima Qian says of the Xiongnu: 'In good times they are accustomed to following their cattle, enjoying field sports and getting drunk; in bad times everyone prepares for war in order to make raids' (*Shiji* 40). Hun raiders, much like their predatory predecessors the Xiongnu, would strike fast and hard, only to disappear in an instant. From China to Europe, sedentary cultures around the steppe-rim had always been at risk of sudden attack by these centaur-like people, who were able to shoot with extraordinary accuracy and power while at full gallop. And so it was with the Xiongnu: 'The Xiongnu move on the feet of swift horses, and in their breasts beat the hearts of beasts. They shift from place to place as swiftly as a flock of birds; so that it is extremely difficult to corner them and bring them under control … it would not be expedient to attack the Xiongnu. Better to make peace with them' (cited in Greer 1975: 24).

This was the advice of a certain Han An-kuo, prime minister to the Han emperor Jingdi (r. 157–141 BC), a circumspect courtier who clearly emphasizes to his master the futility of war against the northern barbarians. Half-a-millennium later, the Huns too inspired terror by the speed of their movements. With two or three horses each, an unencumbered war party could cover some 160km a day over favourable terrain. Thus, with their system of reserve mounts, the Huns could ensure that no messenger travelled faster than they did. As a result the first the occupants of a peaceful settlement learned of the arrival of a hostile band of Huns was probably a cloud of dust, followed by the dull thud of hooves, followed by a rain of arrows.

As Ammianus Marcellinus says of the Huns, 'they are lightly equipped for swiftness and surprise' (AM 31.2.8). For this reason alone it is easy to assume that horse nomads have an inherent superiority over settled peoples in the ability to strike and the ability to subdue. The matter is not that simple, however. Of course, raiding a foreign land is one thing, maintaining control is quite another. The nomad chieftain who marks out any settled region to provide him with tribute, whether he is conquering or merely raiding, sacrifices a part of his initial advantage. He may have to defend his asserted right of rule or plunder against rival nomads. He must therefore establish an advantage of position and in doing so sacrifice at least some of the advantages of mobility. A preoccupation of this kind has further consequences. 'A nomad society that adapts its economy to the acquisition of wealth and power from partly non-nomadic sources must alter its own social structure accordingly. The nature of its new vested interests converts it into something that is no longer a pure nomad society' (Lattimore 1940: 333). Nomadic culture creates jacks-of-all-trades, and every nomad is versed in a variety of skills that allow him to survive in the steppe, but these are not enough for ruling an empire. As Yelü Chucai (Pinyin: *Yēlü Chǔcái*), the Khitan administrative genius to Genghis Khan, would shrewdly

Tibetan archer using a thumb ring, Berlin summer 1938. The thumb ring itself is placed on the thumb of the draw-hand with the bowstring lying in a slight depression in the ring's surface. The hole is oval and not circular, which ensures that the ring sits snugly on the thumb. (Bundesarchiv, Bild 135-S-18-O7-16 / Schäfer, Ernst / CC-BY-SA)

observe seven centuries after Attila, 'a country can be conquered but not governed from the saddle' (Anon. *Yüan-shih* 146). The Mongolian conquests had been breathless and brutal. Even so, Genghis Khan and his successors were to adopt concepts of power and government alien to the traditions of the steppe.

All that was still a long way off at the time of which we are writing, but by building an empire, the Mongols ceased to be genuine nomads. This was true of the Huns before them. A nomad chieftain derived his power from certain aspects of the nomad society, above all, from its mobility. Yet he was tempted to use this power to make himself overlord of a region that yielded rich and easy pickings, in spite of the fact that he thus limited his mobility and undermined the structure of his own power. For a ruler of a steppe people there was a delicate problem of balance between wealth in revenue and advantage in war. With what was his power chiefly concerned – revenue or war? For the European Huns, Attila was to complete the process of making wealth ascendant over mobility.

'The tyrant at table' – Dinner with Attila

Priscus, the author of the fragmentary history, wrote a vivid and detailed first-hand account of a Roman embassy's visit to the court of Attila. He tells us that a feast had been arranged in the palace of Attila, a sprawling wooden affair surrounded by a palisade. Albeit in wood, this was a place designed to impress by the quality of its craftsmanship, for as Priscus says: 'It had been fitted together with highly polished timbers and boards' (fr. 8), whose joints – the addition is from Jordanes – 'so counterfeited solidity that they could scarce be distinguished by close scrutiny'.

Priscus, with his observant eye and retentive memory, describes a spacious wooden hall, beautifully constructed, lit up by great torches of pine, its walls adorned with woven wool wall hangings, its floor with felted wool rugs covered with kilims. Two lines of small tables covered in linen, for the guests and their hosts, had been arranged down each side. The royal table for Attila and members of his family, covered with fine linen, stood in the centre raised on a dais above the level of the rest. In contrast to the side tables, which glittered with gold and silver tableware, presumably taken as plunder on some raid across the Roman frontier, the royal board was graced with simple wooden cups and platters. The Romans were placed on the left-hand row, high-ranking Huns and subject Germanic chieftains on the more honourable right. Each side table accommodated three or four guests.

Attila sits in the middle of a Roman dining couch covered with woven wool carpets. 'A large head, small deep-seated eyes, a flat nose, a thin beard (*rarus baba*), broad shoulders, and a short square body – powerful but ill-proportioned.' So went the pen-portrait of Attila by Jordanes (*Get.* 182 probably from Priscus). Attila, though past middle life, is still full of power and vigour, both physically and mentally, his ruggedness surpassed only by his intelligence. Unlike the non-Roman guests, who are bedecked in barbaric finery gleaming with gold and jewels, Attila is clad in plain skin garments, simple, unadorned, but well kept and spotlessly clean. A Sassanian sword at his left side and a long Sassanian dagger, which is hung horizontally across the abdomen, are both housed in plain, leather scabbards. In his right hand he holds a wooden cup.

To the right of the king's couch, in the place of highest honour, is Onegesius, the king's closest comrade and chief adviser. This noble Hun sits on a Chinese folding chair. He is attired as his king, but all is richly adorned with gilded bronze – the eagle motif being predominant. Likewise, he wears a Sassanian sword but the hilt and scabbard are gilded – it is Priscus who informs us that only the trusted of Attila's friends were armed in his presence. In his right hand is a golden goblet; his left lightly rests upon the hilt of his sword. On his left arm he wears a gold and blood-red garnet armlet. At the left end of the king's couch sits Attila's eldest son Ellac, eyes cast down out of respect for his father. He is attired as his father, likewise plain and simple. He wears no sword, just a dagger.

Attila's career as a consummate raider in all likelihood began under his uncle Ruga, but that as the greatest ruler of the Huns began formally when his brother passed on. In this solo role Attila proved himself to be a ruthless leader with a dangerously great charisma, and a dangerously huge power between the Huns and their subject allies. As such, he demonstrated considerable ability as a super-tribal warlord. His successes, however, were limited. He could lay waste to the Balkan provinces with fire and sword, but he could not penetrate further into his preferred prey, the East Roman Empire. His campaigns were thus pursued in support of a diplomatic policy whose main aim seems to have been the extraction of handsome sums of gold as blackmail.

In AD 435, near the city of Margus in Moesia Superior, Attila (and Bleda) extracted an annual tribute of 700lb of gold (50,400 *solidi*) from the East, which was a doubling of the previous yearly payments to Ruga of 350lb (25,200 *solidi*), along with an agreement to pay 8 *solidi* per head for fugitive Roman prisoners of war. This was the famous occasion when the two brothers proudly refused to dismount, and thereupon forcing the ambassadors from Constantinople, 'mindful of their own dignity' (Prisc. fr. 1), to painfully transact business on horseback. Again in AD 443, when the eastern army had failed to stem his advance, Attila's terms had to be accepted – the immediate payment of 6,000lb of gold (a lump sum of 432,000 *solidi*), and that his annual tribute should be augmented from the previous 700 to 2,100lb of gold (151,200 *solidi*), that is trebled. In addition, every Roman prisoner who escaped from the Huns was now to be ransomed at 12 *solidi* per head and no fugitive from Attila's realm was in future to be received by the Romans (Prisc. fr. 5). To put these figures in some sort of perspective, a *bucellarius* – a Roman commander's armed retainer – was paid around 30 *solidi* per annum (*CTh*. xi.18), while the richest senators had annual incomes of 4,000lb of gold, and middling ones of 1,000 to 1,500lb (Olymp. fr. 44). Set against these figures, 432,000 *solidi* was a vast lump sum.

Presentation of mounted archery, Ópusztaszer, Hungary. The rest of Europe may hate the Huns, but not so the Hungarians, who ambitiously insert the name of the supposedly amiable Attila among their native kings. Almost all Eurasian pastoral nomads were master horsemen and master bowmen, but none matched the Hun in his destructive ability. Yet there was more to mounted archery than bows and arrows. The Hun was fast, bellicose, at one with his horse, and Isidorus Hispalensis (*HV* 29) made a good point when he alluded to him in terms of the mythical creature the centaur. (Csanády)

Some would argue that Attila's fierce love of gold became a sickness of the mind that grew and grew. Greed is a destroyer, and following its trail, a man goes down to defeat. True, his successes had been those of a plunderer, not a potentate, a robber baron, not an empire builder. Yet the eastern emperor Theodosius II bent over backwards to appease Attila, and no one on earth was more agreeably poised to exploit another man's subservience than Attila. Not only did he see Theodosius in these terms – he counted on it. The acquisition of riches from his sedentary neighbour allowed Attila to reward his followers and therefore consolidate and strengthen his position. Peace and friendship never prevailed with Attila unless it was accompanied by the jingling of moneybags containing Roman *solidi*. Nonetheless, Attila may have been accomplished in extracting the proverbial golden eggs, but he took care not to kill the Roman goose that laid them.

Obviously Attila was not alone when it came to enriching oneself on the spoils of a troubled era. Many Huns saw the East Roman Empire as a land of opportunity and were impressed by the ease of urban life, with its seemingly constant supply of luxuries and higher standard of living. They may have detested Rome (viz. Constantinople) as one will often hate a superior, but they also admired it and wanted to become part of a more advanced and wealthy Roman world, a world of wine and warmth and wealth, to enjoy these benefits themselves, preferably on their own terms. Those whose power was based beyond the frontier were greedy for the luxuries they could get from Constantinople, but they were equally anxious to keep their subjects – who had a military value – from being contaminated by Roman ways, let alone be tempted to travel southwards in search of an easier life. Procopius talks of the grievances of one Hun chieftain, complaining to Iustinianus (r. AD 527–65) that refugees from his rule in the empire 'will have the power to traffic in grain, and to get drunk in their wine stores, and to live on the fat of the land … they will be able to go to the baths, and to wear gold ornaments, the villains, and will not go short of fine embroidered cloths' (*Wars* 8.19.16–17, cf. 14). Though a mid 6th-century report, this seems to be more representative of views held by Attila 100 years or so before.

For the European Huns raiding was not only a necessity during times of hardship but became a well-ingrained habit, for as they became more skilled at raiding, they increasingly gave up any attempt at supplementing their subsistence in other ways. Physically tough and logistically mobile, they had the power to rob and, while remaining essentially herders, this inclination led to a permanent state of raiding. The Romans frequently bought them off, which was not difficult to do, as they raided principally for plunder. Without a doubt the Huns, who were quick to take advantage, saw this approach as a sign of imperial weakness.

Gold-hilted sword in a gold scabbard (London, British Museum, inv. ME 135738), said to come from Dailaman, north-west Iran. Despite his fame as a horse archer, the Hun was also known for the long, double-edged sword hitched at his waist, and he knew how to use it. The sword's exceptional length increased the reach and power of the mounted warrior. Surviving examples have much in common with Sassanian swords from Iran, as seen here. The sword was hung obliquely from a loose sword-belt, which rested on the hips. The hip-belt derives from a Sassanian type in which the belt runs through an elongated scabbard-slide on the outer face of the weapon's scabbard. This system suits the mounted warrior but makes the weapon difficult to draw when on foot. (British Museum)

Let us assume, therefore, Hun raiders hoped to gain as much plunder as possible and then retire without undue fuss. The plunder taken by them tended to be confined to easily movable items, and most raids did not penetrate very deep into Roman territory. Relying on no more than the composite bow and a string of horses, raiding parties were small, lightly loaded and fast moving. Having penetrated the Roman frontier they usually remained dispersed, but often concentrated if a Roman field army (*comitatus*) entered the area of operations. Nevertheless, raids were not intended to be bloody affairs but a means of acquiring plunder by stealth. The return journey was made as rapidly as possible, despite the acquisition of booty, and by travelling without rest or sleep the raiders usually made a successful escape. They avoided fighting at all costs. In direct contrast, large-scale military activity depended upon effective leadership. The European Huns mounted major attacks against the East Roman Empire in AD 441, 443 and 447, and in AD 451 and 452 they attacked the West Roman Empire. However, these high-level operations were only feasible because of the unification of the various trans-Danubian tribes, both Hun and non-Hun alike, under a single capable leader, Attila.

ABOVE

Byzantine *spangenhelm* (Mainz, Mittelrheinisches Landesmuseum), found in Bad Kreuznach-Planig, Tomb 1, and dated first-third of 6th century AD. Made from strips of iron (the *spangen*) forming a framework, to which leaf-shaped iron plates were attached internally. (akg-images)

RIGHT

Modern reconstruction of lamellar body armour. Of Asiatic origin, lamellar armour was made of *lamellae*, small vertical plates of polished bone or horn laced together with leather thongs. Lamellar would have been fairly stiff and inflexible, requiring additional *pteruges* at the vulnerable groin and armpits. (Kimball)

THE HOUR OF DESTINY

The chronology for Attila's campaigns in the AD 440s are always going to be problematical, particularly so when our chief Anglophone authorities, Thompson and Maenchen-Helfen, differ, but it must be remembered that the relevant sources are fragmentary and the dates uncertain.

In AD 441, taking advantage of the fact that the Persians had recently launched an invasion of Roman Armenia and a huge naval expedition had sailed from Constantinople to rescue Carthage from the Vandals (PT *ad annum* 441), Attila crossed the Danubius. Having chosen his time so well, throughout the nine-month campaign (summer AD 441 to spring AD 442) Attila met with no opposition from the eastern field armies (*comitatensis*), they being otherwise engaged of course, and the cities of Margus (Dubrovica), Viminacium (Koštolac), Singidunum (Belgrade) and Sirmium (Sremska Mitrovica) were razed to the ground and their inhabitants enslaved. An enormous hole had been punched in the fortifications of the middle Danube frontier, and the Balkan provinces lay at the mercy of the Huns.

When the campaigning season of AD 443 came around, Attila duly laid waste to the Balkans and one of his victims was the great Balkan city of Serdica (Sofia). Next, in a rapid succession of battles near Constantinople, Attila defeated the eastern field army (*comitatus*), which was then commanded by Aspar, with deplorable ease. The Hun threat to the capital seemed real enough at the time, whatever historians may say with hindsight today. A metropolis of incomparable wealth and splendour, many must have feared that the Huns would only rein in their horses when Constantinople too was an empty smoking ruin.

Terracotta tomb figurine of a Toba warrior on a caparisoned horse (Paris, Musée Cernuschi, inv. MC 7244), Northern Wei dynasty (AD 386–534). Lamellar armour was much more effective against arrows than mail, and in addition to this protection, steppe warriors also preferred it because of its simplicity of manufacture. Equine armour had long been the characteristic of the elite riders of the Eurasian steppes, namely the tribal chieftain and his personal retainers. Such armour was of iron *lamellae* or felt, and the main problem facing an armoured horse was heat exhaustion, not weight. (Guillaume Jacquet)

Siege of Naissus

Another of Attila's notable victims of AD 443 was the city of Naissus (Niš) in Dacia Mediterranea, birthplace of Constantine the Great and seat of a state-run armaments factory or *fabrica*, which turned out all sorts of military hardware. This city was, and has long been, an important nodal point, commanding, as it does, two river valleys that lead out of central Europe towards the Aegean. But it was not easily defensible, as Attila was about to prove.

Normally the Huns were not trained or eager for siege warfare, but Priscus' literary description (fr. 1b) of the siege of Naissus clearly illustrates how urbane Hunnic warfare had become. The city lay on the right bank of the river now called the Nišava. The Huns bridged the river to enable them to bring their siege machines close to the circuit wall. These were 'wooden beams mounted

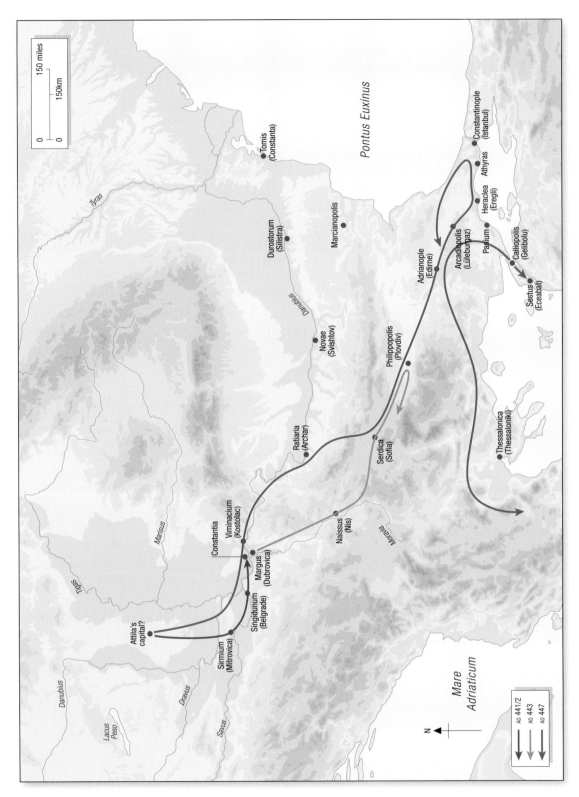

on wheels', on which men perched to fire arrows at those defending the battlements. These warriors were protected by screens made of woven willow and rawhide, thick and heavy enough to stop incoming missiles, but with slits through which they could fire. The Huns also brought forward rams. Each consisted of a beam with a metal head that was suspended by chains from timbers inclined towards each other. Further screens protected the operators. Priscus describes the mechanics: using small ropes attached to a projection at the rear, the operators forcibly drew the beam backwards and then let go so that it swung forwards to strike the wall in front.

The defenders themselves were not idle. The besiegers were assailed by fire darts and 'stones by the waggon load'. But to no avail. The city wall was breached through the sheer number of rams and the Huns gained entry. Some six years later, when the diplomatic mission of which Priscus was a member, passed through Naissus on the way to the court of Attila, the city was still a scene of desolation. Halting near by the Nišava, Priscus observed that 'every place on the bank was full of bones of those slain in the war' (fr. 8).

It can be taken for granted that prisoners were compelled to build the siege machines, presumably under the direction of Roman engineers, who were either conscripted or served the Huns as free agents – Attila warmly welcomed turncoats and made full use of their familiarity with 'modern technology'. We can also surmise that prisoners were also forced to take an active part in the siege. They would have been made to dig trenches and erect defences and to undertake whatever other thankless tasks were deemed necessary. They would have even worked the rams under heavy fire, while others were made to carry the Huns' long scaling ladders up to the very walls. If prisoners tried to run away, they would have been put to death. Thus, they had a choice of certain death at the hands of the Huns or probable death at the hands of the defenders of Naissus. Often those defenders manning the crumbling walls of the city must have recognized their own kith and kin among the prisoners below.

The Huns of Attila, by the Spanish artist Ulpiano Checa y Sanz (1860–1916). Attila (right, foreground), at the head of his apocalyptic horse warriors, sweeps into Italy. In western psyche the sickening scent of sulphur and the heat of the hellish flames still envelope the Huns, a demonization first articulated by late antique chroniclers, a habit that continues to this day. (© Bridgeman Art Library)

Riding roughshod over Europe

In AD 447, favoured by recent earthquakes that devastated Asia Minor, Attila, now sole ruler, marched on Constantinople itself, the walls of which had suffered severe damage. According to Priscus (fr. 43 = CM *ad annum* 447), these massive land walls, including no less than 57 of its 96 towers, fell to the ground. Fortunately for the East Roman Empire the fortifications were repaired and strengthened just before the arrival of the Huns (*ILS* 823). The mighty walls of Constantinople could once again withstand the worse assault an assailant could hurl against them, and the hard-riding Huns turned aside and drove down southwards into Greece and came as far as Thermopylae. As *comes* Marcellinus (no relation of Ammianus Marcellinus) vigorously writes for his entry under the year AD 447, 'Attila ground almost the whole of Europe into dust' (CM *ad annum* 447).

On 28 July AD 450, when out riding, Theodosius II fell from his horse and broke his back. He died soon afterwards. The succession was smooth, it being quietly accomplished by the marriage of Pulcheria, his sister, to Marcianus (r. AD 450–57), who thereupon assumed the purple. But the West showed an initial reluctance to recognize the new emperor of the East. And he in return contrived, deliberately or otherwise, to divert the hostile Hun from East to West, by ending the ruinous tribute payments to Attila, apparently saying, 'I have gold for my friends, and iron for my enemies.'

The West could afford to pay an annual tribute even less, and in early AD 451 Attila turned his gaze westward and made the decision to invade Gaul. He had been given a pretext to do so when Honoria, sister of Valentinianus III and daughter of Galla Placidia, driven into paroxysms of rage over an arranged marriage forced upon her, sent her signet ring to Attila, urging the king to come to her rescue (IA fr. 199.2). Professing to interpret this as an offer of marriage, with splendid panache Attila demanded 'Valentinianus

dampede·

Do dehunen even her

Attila's death by haemorrhaging during his wedding night was an extraordinary ending to his adventurous life. In the 14th-century *Saxon Chronicle of the World* (Berlin, Staatsbiliothek, Ms. Germ. 129 f. 53), the dying Attila is portrayed not as an ungodly pagan marauder but as a pious Christian monarch. (Scala)

should withdraw from half of the empire in his favour' (Prisc. fr. 16) as her dowry. Of course there are those who dismiss out of hand this story of the Roman princess and the barbarian king as Byzantine court gossip and thus unworthy of belief. But demanding a Roman princess in marriage implied diplomatic recognition on an equal footing.

Shortly thereafter Placidia died, and her otiose son Valentinianus was left alone to decide what next – it appears only the females among the Theodosian family inherited the founder's strength of character. Not knowing how to handle the Hun, for Attila's demand truly frightened him and it could be argued that his feebleness was more a matter of cowardice, the pampered Valentinianus turned to the complaisant Roman warlord Aëtius for help, who was obviously of the opinion that it was pointless trying to avert a war that had already broken out. When his demand was eventually refused, Attila decided to march westward. With that, as Gibbon declared, 'the kings and nations of Germany and Scythia, from the Volga perhaps to the Danube, obeyed the warlike summons of Attila' (*D&F*, chap. XXXV, p. 405). In the spring of AD 451, Attila and his army crossed the Rhenus (Rhine) and penetrated into the heart of Gaul, only to be thwarted outside Aurelianum (Orléans) and then defeated at the Catalaunian Plains by a western coalition army under Aëtius.

The Tisza at Tiszapüspöki, Hungary. This is probably the river Priscus calls the Tigas, somewhere between which and the Danubius (Danube) Attila had his wooden capital. (Lily 15)

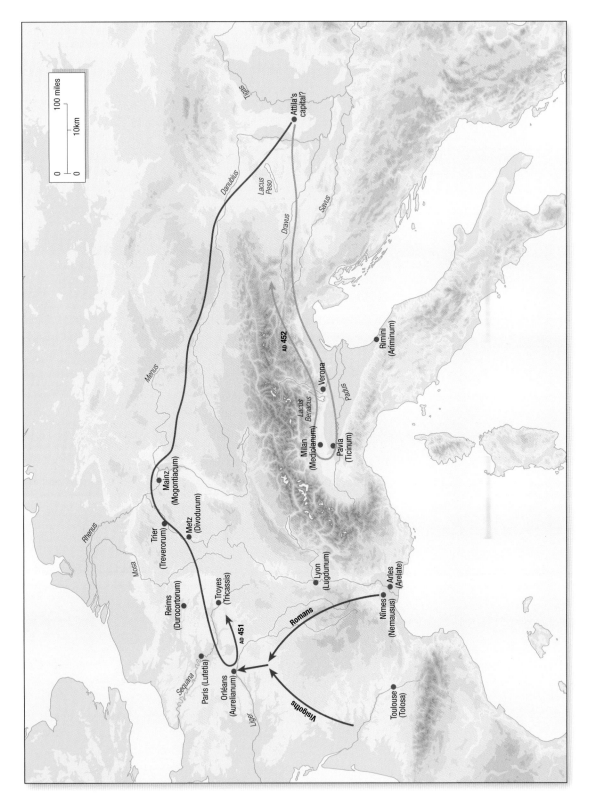

The Catalaunian Plains

Attila and his army crossed the Rhenus along a wide front and swept into central Gaul towards Lutetia (Paris) and then Aurelianum. Lutetia was apparently saved by the prayers and fasting of a young virgin, now remembered as St Geneviève, but the more important city of Aurelianum was invested. Had he gained his objective, Attila would have been in a strong position to subdue the Visigoths in Aquitania Secunda, but Aëtius put together a formidable coalition for the defence of Gaul. Traditionally foes of the Romans, his newfound barbarian allies – Visigoths, Alans, Burgundians and Salian Franks – were nonetheless wedded to Aëtius' cause through a common hatred (and fear) of Attila. Hence, at the Catalaunian Plains, Aëtius' army was very much a barbarian confederation. We use the term 'barbarian' here to describe all of the foreign enemies of the two empires, even though many of them had made considerable advances in civilization, particularly under stimulus of their contacts with the Romans themselves.

BELOW
Panoramic view of Niš, ancient Naissus. (Aleksić Ivan)

LEFT
Late Roman gateway, which pierces the eastern circuit of Naissus. Of strategic importance – five Roman roads met here, including the Via Militaris, which ran 670 Roman miles (992km) from Singidunum to Constantinople – the city lay on the right bank of the river Nišava in the province of Dacia Mediterranea. As the principal city of said province, it was the seat of a state-run arms factory and was thickly populated (AM 21.10.5). Its fortifications had been strengthened by Iulianus (the Apostate). When the Huns rode away from it in AD 443, the birthplace of Constantine the Great lay desolated until Iustinianus restored it in the following century. (Novak Watchman)

Attila for his part, however, did not lack friends. Roman North Africa lay almost beyond the horizon of Hunnic history, but not quite, for Geiseric (r. AD 428–77), king of the Vandals, had already played a role in the prelude to the battle. A crippled son of an anonymous slave, Geiseric was a proud pitiless leader, a gifted conspirator with a genius for political intrigue. 'He was a man of deep thought and few words', wrote Jordanes, 'holding luxury in disdain, furious in anger, greedy for gain, shrewd in winning over the Barbarians and skilled in sowing the seeds of discord among his enemies' (*Get.* 168). For 50 years his web of entangling treaties would foil the plans of Roman diplomats and fellow barbarian rulers.

In this way the subtle Geiseric had urged Attila to attack the Visigoths because of the enmity between Vandal and Visigoth. Geiseric's son Huneric had married the unnamed daughter of the Visigoth king Theodoric (r. AD 418–51), who was the son of Alaric (SA *PA* 505). However, in the summer of AD 442 Valentinianus, the third of that name, emperor of the West, agreed to the betrothal of his daughter Eudocia to Geiseric's son. At the time she was just three years old. The Visigoth princess was thus sent back to her father's court at Tolosa, her nose and ears inhumanly mutilated, thus despoiling her natural beauty and nullifying her political value. Rumour had it she was suspected of involvement in a plot to poison Geiseric (Jord. *Get.* 184). In the cutthroat world of court politics, rumour quite readily substitutes for fact. It seems more likely that the wily Geiseric was moved by his eagerness to bring about this betrothal between his son and the Roman princess. Unsurprisingly, when Attila crossed the Rhenus, the Visigoths joined Aëtius, but the Vandals stayed out of the war.

Attila had not expected such vigorous action on the part of Aëtius, and the king was too wise to allow his army to be trapped outside the walls of Aurelianum, so he raised the siege (14 June) and sought open spaces and

Reconstruction of Constantinople and its impregnable defences. The city was built on a hilly promontory, surrounded on three sides by water with fast-flowing currents, which made it difficult to attack from the sea, an option hardly open to the Huns in any case. On the landward side, it was sealed off by a triple line of defences, the most important of which was the inner wall 5m thick at its base and 4.5m thick at its apex and punctuated by 96 towers. No enemy ever breached this barrier until Mehmet II took the city in 1453 using the latest military technology, gunpowder weapons. Attila, 1,000 years before, was granted a chance to do so when, in the dark hours of the early morning of Sunday, 27 January AD 447, a severe earthquake reduced the walls to jumble heaps of brick and stone. (© Nic Fields)

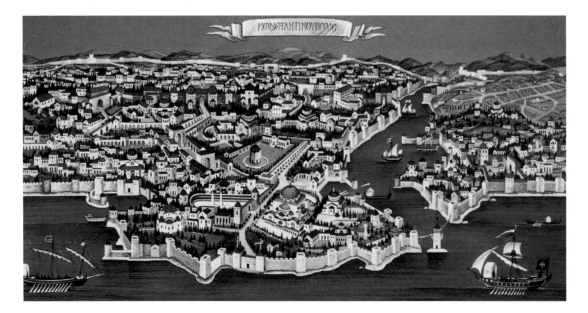

fast progress. The excellent general, as Sun Tzu saw it, chooses the ground on which he wishes to engage, draws his enemy to it, and there gives battle. To Sun Tzu (10.8–9), the military genius of Warring States China, a general unable to use ground properly was unfit to command. Attila would have not known of Sun Tzu's book of war, but he did have a special feeling for nature and an appreciation of the influences terrain always has on strategy. With that, Attila made for open grasslands to the north-east where he could use his horse-riding warriors to best advantage. 'The nations from the Volga to the Atlantic', writes Gibbon, 'were assembled on the plain of Châlons' (*D&F*, chap. XXXV, p. 411).

On the morning of 20 June the imperial army deployed with the Romans, under Aëtius, on the left flank, and the Visigoths, under the aged Theodoric, on the right. The Alans occupied the centre under Sangiban, a king whose loyalty to any cause but his own preservation was considered highly doubtful by Aëtius (Jord. *Get*. 196, cf. 194). Sandwiching Sangiban between himself and Theodoric appeared the best way to control the dubious Alan loyalty. Nine years previously, Aëtius had settled these Alans near Aurelianum so as to keep an eye on the neighbouring territory of the *tractus Armoricanus* (modern Brittany), the home of the Bacaudae, 'an inexperienced and disorderly band of rustics' (Oros. 7.25.2). As *foederati*, treaty troops, the Alans were bound to serve whenever and wherever they were called, but their main and permanent assignment was to defend themselves. By fighting for their new home, they fought for Rome too. Yet when Attila made camp outside Aurelianum, it seems that Sangiban was planning a quick and treacherous shift of loyalty (Jord. *Get*. 194).

Attila's army is said to have numbered 500,000 men (Jord. *Get*. 182), though this is doubtless a gross exaggeration, and actually it cannot have had more than a fifth of this figure, and probably even less. Anyway, on the right wing of his army Attila stationed the Gepids under his most reliable ally, Ardaric, along with the bulk of his other Germanic allies. The Ostrogoths, under their king Valamer, took the left opposite their distant cousins the Visigoths, and in the centre Attila placed the best and bravest of his army, the Huns. All in all, it was a curious ethnographical collection, an *omnium gatherum*, which stood that day on the Catalaunian Plains.

The battlefield itself was a large level area of 'one hundred *leuva* in length … and seventy in width' (*c*.300 acres, Jord. *Get*. 192), cut by a stream and rising

The Theodosian walls of Constantinople, looking north-west towards the triple line of defences between the Golden Gate (right) and the Second Military Gate (left). On its landward side the city was guarded by an impregnable edifice that ran the 6.5km from the Propontis (Sea of Marmara) to the Golden Horn, in large measure impressively intact today. In this particular stretch all the 11 towers that guard the inner wall are still standing, as all but one of those in the outer wall: a tribute to Roman engineering genius. However, little remains of the moat; apart from this section here, it has mostly been filled in. (© Nic Fields)

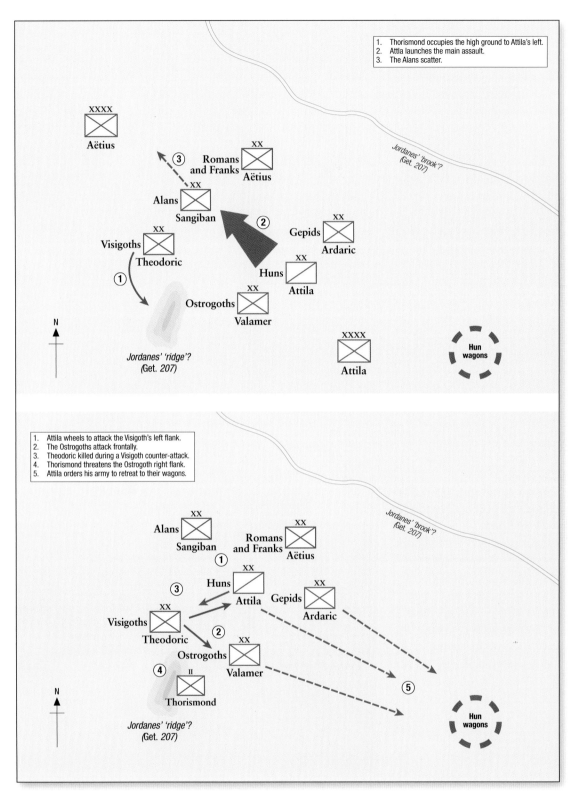

nearby in one of the ocean-plain's slight billows. Documentary evidence for the engagement is in fact very thin, the only extensive account being that of Jordanes (*Get.* 197–213). He tells us that before the main battle was joined, Theodoric apparently dispatched his son Thorismond to occupy the soft billow, which happened to overlook the left flank of the Huns. Attila responded by detaching some troops to drive away Thorismond, but these, in their effort to gain the summit, were easily routed. Both kings were veterans of numerous engagements and encounters – between them there were 60 long years of soldiering – and Theodoric and Attila used this experience to advantage by quickly attempting to seize what high ground there was. Yet the real fighting had scarcely begun.

Attila, casting aside the usual Hun tactic of first softening up the opposition with missile fire, launched his forces straight at the coalition army. In an allegorical speech to his men, Attila is supposed to have said the following: 'The Romans are poor soldiers, keeping together in rank and file. They are contemptible, the only worthy enemies are the Alans and the Visigoths' (Jord. *Get.* 204).

Egg-tempera on wood icon (Athens, private collection), provenance unknown, 18th century. The image shows the siege of Constantinople by the Turkic Avars in AD 626. Like the Huns before them, the Turkic Avars, who are depicted here as Ottoman Turks, were Inner Asian horse warriors and shared the Huns' grand ambitions and ruthless drive. The destruction of the city by the Avars was averted only by the military skills of the soldier emperor Heraclius (r. AD 610–41), or, as was otherwise claimed and clearly alluded to in this icon, the Blessed Virgin Mary. (© Nic Fields)

With their highly developed tactic of rapid-fire barrage shooting, the usual opening manoeuvre was for the Huns to wear down the enemy from a distance. Thus, successive bands of horsemen would advance, wheel and retreat (viz. the 'Parthian shot'), shooting volleys of arrows from the saddle as they did so. The latter would be done at high elevation, a skill developed by steppe dwellers, which meant arrows would land almost vertically on a predetermined area target. Each successive band would relieve the one before to keep up an incessant barrage. This skirmishing would continue until the enemy was sufficiently weakened or demoralized. It was then that they would close in for the decisive encounter.

Given the right conditions of course, the Huns preferred, and most profitable, battlefield tactic was to try to envelop the flank or rear of their foe; here their strengths of speed, mobility and firepower were exploited to the full.

All things being equal, this is how it usually worked. Riding at full gallop and parallel with the static line of the enemy, the archer turns in his saddle and fires sideways – the arrow flying almost flat – reloads, fires again, and again, all within a few seconds. The archer's technique here would be to release his shot when the horse is in full flight, hooves off *terra firma*, he himself tensing his body on the draw, relaxing on the release. So as to fire one arrow after another at speed he does not resort to the quiver – that is only to store arrows – but holds a bunch of arrows – six, seven, maybe as many as nine depending on his skill and experience – in his left hand against the outer edge of the bow and spread like an array of playing cards. The bow and arrow have got one of the fastest arming recycle times of any pre-modern projectile weapon, but this toxophilites trick allows these arrows to be fired off much sooner than it takes to write this paragraph on the keyboard.

At the Catalaunian Plains, however, it was not to be so.

Whereas in wide-open spaces the Huns were without peer, with the battle lines so extended there was little opportunity for them to try their preferred encircling trick. Progress was therefore limited, aside from a frontal attack. So Attila concentrated his main attack, using his best warriors, the Huns, in the centre. This was where Aëtius had posted the untrustworthy Sangiban, more cunning than loyal, where his Alans had no choice but to stand fast and fight. Yet in spite of the wavering Alans scattering on the Huns' initial charge, the battle was hard fought, lasting for most of the day with heavy casualties on both sides. In his dramatic description of the battle Jordanes (*Get.* 208) has the local stream run crimson with blood, while the battlefield itself was a charnel ground.

Theodoric was amongst the slain, trampled to death by his own Visigoths as he was urging them on or (as some said) transfixed by the spear of Andag,

'Where his horse had trod' – Attila at the Catalaunian Plains

Attila has lifted his siege of Aurelianum and moved northwards to an arena that, topographically, might be styled a great undulating plain, rolling like the waves of an ocean – a sea of grass, over which he could use his horse warriors to profitable effect. Yet strangely, when the fighting started, it was a straightforward pounding-match, with no elaborate tactics. Victory would go to the side that stood and did not flinch. With the battle lines so extended there was little opportunity for the Huns to try their preferred encircling trick. So Attila concentrated his main attack, using his best troops, the Huns, in the centre. Here Aëtius had stationed the unreliable Sangiban and his Alans, where they had no choice but to stand fast and fight.

In this reconscruction the Huns roll across the grassy ground between the armies in an accelerating tide, and despite their lack of formal organization, they behave as though animated by a collective will. The riders in the van have wheeled left and right when a hundred paces from the Alan front, and are now galloping parallel to the enemy, discharging dense clouds of arrows. Their place is about to be taken by the next wave of bow warriors, so that the scene will resolve itself into two vast whirlpools of horsemen swirling in front of the static ranks of Sangiban's warriors.

The Huns, controlling their charging mounts with thigh and knee, continuously fit arrows to the strings of their bows. To enable rapid fire, additional arrows are held in the bow hand. The Alan king knows that so long as his warriors keep formation protected by their shields, the mounted foe would not press home a charge against an array of spear points. It was not to be. The front ranks, the warriors wearing both helmets and hauberks, and with enough room to raise their shields, remain relatively unscathed. But the warriors in the middle ranks, helmeted but lacking body armour, and so close-packed they are unable to use their shields to protect their upper bodies, are beginning to suffer terrible punishment from the Hun barrage. The Alan ranks thin steadily under the effects of the brisk attack.

Normally, Attila does not take part in the battle. However, today is different. Helmeted and armoured and surrounded by his retinue (*comitatus*) of armoured horse warriors, men specially selected for their courage, skill, iron discipline and unbending loyalty, the king of the Huns (we see him holding his spear vertically aloft) has taken the field at the head of his Huns, armed to the teeth in all the panoply of grim Hunnic war, and bent on destruction and victory. The Alan king stands in the third rank of his warriors, nervously watching the Hun van as it sweeps down. He is about to get a close look at the Hun king's fearlessness.

a noble Ostrogoth, but nightfall saw the coalition army in possession of the field. Attila had pulled back his exhausted and battered forces into his wagon laager, thus preparing for a fight to the death on the following day. Jordanes would have us believe that Attila, determined not to be taken alive, piled saddles within his wagon circle to form a pyre upon which he would fling himself if need be. But Aëtius, fearing his new allies the Visigoths scarcely less than his former friends the Huns, forbore from destroying a possible counterpoise to their power (Jord. *Get*. 216). He therefore urged Thorismond to return post-haste with his forces to his kingdom's capital at Tolosa and thereupon secure his position on the throne. Doubtless the strong Visigoth performance on the Catalaunian Plains would have been of some concern to Aëtius, in that it could have encouraged the new king to believe an alliance with the West Roman Empire was unneeded. To all sense and purposes, Aëtius had let Attila off the hook and allowed the Huns to withdraw unmolested (Thompson 1948: 142–3). It had been a close-run thing on the Catalaunian Plains.

Ironically this battle has been reckoned as one of the most decisive in world history (Creasy et al.), the battle that saved western Europe from Attila and his terrible Huns. This sounds quite plausible, but it is not true. Granted, the Catalaunian Plains was the West Roman Empire's greatest (albeit final) triumph. Yet considering its violence, it decided very little, and was at best a stalemate. Both sides sustained immense losses and neither were really victorious. Keeping his battered multi-tribal army intact, Attila retreated to his wooden capital on the Hungarian grasslands and the next spring launched a major offensive into Italy itself.

OPPOSING COMMANDERS

On the basis of laconic, scattered texts, we can only assume that Attila fought a wide variety of opponents, both Roman and non-Roman alike. Obviously it is the Roman opponents that we know about, and of those Flavius Aëtius and Flavius Aspar stand out above the rest. Incidentally, true Flavii were rare, whereas it was usual for an imperial servant to use the dynastic title 'Flavius', to which he was entitled, and his last name only. Hence, the proliferation of the *praenomen* Flavius in late antiquity, e.g. Stilicho, Gaudentius, Felix, Aëtius, Aspar, Belisarius, etc.

Flavius Aëtius (AD 391–454)

The 'last of the Romans', as Procopius (*Wars* 3.3.16) described him, along with his hated rival Bonifatius, Flavius Aëtius was born in Durostorum (Silistra), Moesia Secunda, the son of Flavius Gaudentius, a Roman general of 'Scythian' (viz. possibly Gothic) descent who had risen to the rank of *magister equitum* before being struck down by mutinous Gallic soldiers. An expert political climber, the son was destined to rise to even greater heights.

On the death of Bonifatius, Aëtius gained profound influence over the court in Ravenna, and thereupon thrice securing the consulship (AD 432, 437, 446), an unprecedented distinction for one who was not of the imperial house. Appointed to the rank of patrician (*patricius*, a title now denoting a generalissimo) in AD 433, he became the effective ruler of the West, holding absolute power for more than two decades. Rightly it was said that envoys were no longer sent to Valentinianus III, but directly to Aëtius at his military headquarters, wherever it happened to be, thereby bypassing the court in Ravenna. In AD 434, after successes in Gaul against the Visigoths and the Franks, Aëtius was appointed *magister utriusque militiae*. In the dog-eat-dog world of Roman power politics, fools did not become top generals, nor did paragons of gentle forbearance. Aëtius was surely a firm believer in that ancient adage 'if you don't take power, another will'.

Like Stilicho (related to the imperial family both through his wife and his daughters) and Constantius (through marriage) before him, Aëtius schemed to link his family to the royal line of Theodosius by the marriage of his son Gaudentius with Valentinianus' daughter Eudocia. But this contributed to his startling downfall. One day (21 September AD 454), while Aëtius was presenting a piece of legislation at the palace, Valentinianus suddenly sprang from his throne and accused him of treason. He then drew a concealed sword – 'the first sword he had ever drawn' in the overheated words of Gibbon (*D&F*, chap. XXXV, p. 424). At this point, the usually compliant and cowardly emperor rushed upon

The gilded ridge helmet from Deurne (Leiden, Rijksmuseum van Oudheden, inv. K 1911/4.1-5), Noord-Brabant, discovered in a peat bog in 1910 and dated to *c.*AD 319–23 from the coins found with it. It carries two inscriptions, one giving the name of the maker, M(arcvs) TITVS LVNAMIS, followed by the weight of silver (nearly 370g) he used, and the other stating that the owner belonged to STABLESIA(na) VI, a *vexillatio comitatensis equites sextiae Stablesiana* mentioned in the *Notitia Dignitatum*. This document tells us that there were 15 such *equites Stablesiani* units, seven in the East and eight in the West. (Rob Koopman)

the defenceless man, who was simultaneously attacked by the eunuch Heraclius, the emperor's personal chamberlain and evil genius, and fell lifeless at their feet (IA fr. 201.2).

The last emperor of any dynasty is often vicious and weak – as weak as the founder of the dynasty was ruthless. Valentinianus, the third and last of that name, was no exception to this simple rule. 'The thing, scarce man, Placidia's fatuous son, butchered Aëtius', wrote the sickened Sidonius Apollinaris, and when asked to sanction the murder, one of Valentinianus' courtiers honestly replied, 'you have acted like a man who cuts off his right hand with his left' (PA 359, cf. IA fr. 200.1). Valentinianus, who presumably preferred being told what he wanted to hear from toadying courtiers not candid ones, was to reap the fruits of his own folly. The following year (16 March), while he amused himself in the Campus Martius with the spectacle of some military sports, the emperor was treacherously assassinated in his own turn by two of Aëtius' *bucellarii*. Their names were Optila and Thraustila, and fittingly they were Huns (IA fr. 201.4–5).

The contemptible Valentinianus would not be missed. But the loss of Aëtius was profound. Deprived of the strong leadership 'of the great safety of the Western Empire' (CM *ad annum* 454), as a terse entry in the Latin chronicle of *comes* Marcellinus describes Aëtius, that empire entered its deathly decline. A fair summary, and correct as far as it goes.

Before rising to the dizzy heights of power, Aëtius had experienced many vicissitudes. As a youth he had spent some time as a hostage of the Visigoths, and then of the Huns too, acquiring valuable insight into the

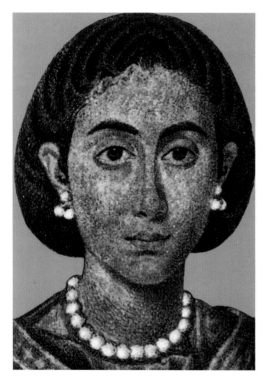

Miniature painting on gilded glass medallion (Brescia, Museo Civico Cristiano), depicting (possibly) Galla Placidia (AD 392–450), daughter, sister, wife and mother of emperors. The daughter of the intolerant Theodosius I and half-sister of the ineffective Honorius, Placidia was destined to lead an out-of-the-ordinary life. Married twice, first in AD 414 to the Visigoth king Ataulf, and second in AD 417 to the Roman generalissimo Constantius, co-emperor of the West for just seven months in AD 421. It was this marriage that catapulted her into power, and she was to remain for a long time the most powerful figure in the West. (© Nic Fields)

leading non-Roman peoples of his day. With the Huns in particular, he learnt much about their customs and established ties of friendship with their nobility. Later chroniclers note his fine sense of horsemanship and expert handling of bow and spear. 'His intelligence was keen and he was full of energy', writes Renatus Frigeridus, 'a superb horseman, a fine shot with an arrow and tireless with the spear'. On the Hungarian steppe, Aëtius learned also the ability to withstand hardship. 'He bore adversity with great patience and was ready for any exacting enterprise' continues Frigeridus, 'he scorned danger and was able to endure hunger, thirst and loss of sleep' (Frigeridus *apud* GT 2.8). Melodramatic myth-building maybe, but Aëtius indisputably understood the Hun art of war (SA *Carm.* 7.230). With the Huns he would remain friendly for a long time, and his path in life was repeatedly to cross that of Attila. Sometime after AD 435, at the time of the joint rule of Bleda and Attila, Aëtius' eldest son Carpilio would follow in his father's footsteps by serving as a hostage on the *puszta* (Prisc. fr. 8, Cass. *Var.* 1.4.11). It is important to bear in mind too that Aëtius' power was not so much on his military ability, which was undeniably great, as on the close relations that he had cemented with the European Huns. Aetius' military successes were entirely due to his ability to hire Hun auxiliaries.

In late August AD 423 Honorius died without issue, and this immediately created a power vacuum. There is little positive that can be said about his reign; he came to the throne a child and always remained a child. Even so, he had managed to stay on the western throne for 28 years. The Emperor of the East and Honorius' nephew, the equally weak and pliable Theodosius II, renounced his previous claim to the western throne, backing instead the next legitimate heir, Valentinianus, the 4-year-old-spoilt son of Aelia Galla Placidia (AD 392–450), Honorius' half-sister, and Constantius, who had reigned for a few months as Constantius III. The sudden death of her husband came as no surprise, but it had aroused a sense of scandal in court circles, particularly regarding Placidia, who had never wanted to marry her brother's chief warlord. 'So great had grown the affection of Honorius for his own sister', rumoured one contemporaneous palace pen-pusher, 'that their immoderate passion and their continuous kissing on the mouth brought them under a shameful suspicion in the eyes of many people' (Olymp. fr. 40).

Court politics soon brought an end to that. Fighting broke out in the streets of Ravenna between the barbarian bodyguard of Placidia and the *scholae palatinae* of the emperor. An appropriate reminder that Placidia was not without power and influence of her own. Before her marriage to Constantius, she had been the wife of the Visigoth king Ataulf (r. AD 410–15). Having spent some five years among the Visigoths, she came to admire them and trusted her protection to a private army of Visigoth *bucellarii* (Prisc. fr. 38). This gave her independence. Not surprisingly, Honorius banished Placidia and her son to Constantinople in AD 423 (Olymp. fr. 40). A few months later, Honorius was dead (27 August). With Placidia and Valentinianus in Constantinople and no other member of the Theodosian dynasty at hand, the western throne was up for grabs.

In AD 424, when Attila was reaching maturity and Aëtius was still holding the modest position of *cura palatii*, the Roman raised a large force of Huns for the usurper Ioannes, an obscure civil servant who had proclaimed himself emperor at Ravenna (Olymp. fr. 41, IA fr. 195). Though Ioannes was not a soldier, but a civilian, Aëtius had agreed to back him because he was anxious to prevent Placidia coming to power as guardian and regent for her son during his years of minority. Ioannes' power, such as it was, lasted only 18 months. His end was both ridiculous and gruesome. He was grossly ridiculed and gruesomely mutilated, after which he was placed on an ass and exposed to jeering mobs as he was ignominiously led through the streets of Aquileia, where he was eventually beheaded (*Wars* 3.3.9).

Right leaf of the consular ivory diptych (Paris, Cabinet des médailles de la BNF, inv. 55 n° 295) of Flavius Constantius Felix. The first man Galla Placidia chose to be her supreme military commander was neither Bonifatius nor Aëtius, possibly fearing that by choosing one she would stir up trouble for herself with the other, but Felix (AD 380–430). He was *magister utriusque militiae* for four years (AD 425–29) and consul in AD 428, but despite a brief mention of one of his military actions in the *Notitia Dignitatum* he does not seem to have taken the field, unlike his subordinates Bonifatius and Aëtius. (Clio20)

Aëtius was not idle. Having entered northern Italy three days after Ioannes had been decapitated, and therefore too late to save him from his fate, Aëtius' own position was for a time precarious. It was then Aëtius decided to further his own cause (if he had not done so already), and with that used the Huns (though not the 60,000 mentioned in later sources) under his command to make his position almost unassailable. It was on this wave of military threat that Aëtius rode to high office. Placidia, now guardian and regent for the boy emperor Valentinianus III (r. AD 425–55), had no option but to employ her former opponent, who 'received the rank of *comes*' (Philo. 12.14, cf. Frigeridus *apud* GT 2.8). Aëtius' Huns departed peacefully after receiving a generous payment of gold.

Placidia, who neither forgot nor forgave that he had supported Ioannes' coup d'état, kept Aëtius in Italy, but gave Bonifatius the military command in the Diocese of Africa, source of Rome's principal grain supply, where Moorish rebels were causing problems. Placidia was a wise woman, keeping her enemy near enough to touch, her friend at a distance. A curious blend of saint and freebooter, the new *comes domesticorum et Africae* was a firm friend of Placidia. Hard men in hard times, Aëtius and Bonifatius were unavoidably potent rivals, and conflict between the two was inevitable. But Bonifatius was having troubles of his own, and in AD 427 Placidia was persuaded to recall him to Ravenna to explain his failures. He refused to obey (IA fr. 196).

A Roman warlord protected by two of his armed retainers, detail from the late 4th-century Great Hunt mosaic at Piazza Armerina, Sicily. Many of the most important military figures in the two empires of this period, such as Stilicho, Aëtius and Aspar, as would Belisarius three generations later, maintained retinues of armed supporters, most visibly in the form of the *bucellarii*. In effect private armies – Belisarius' would number over 1,000 – *bucellarii* could be relied upon to follow their Roman commanders wherever they went. (© Nic Fields)

In AD 429 Bonifatius, after defeating and absorbing her army, called in the aid of the Vandals with the threat of a second Placidian army (*Wars* 3.3.22–26, Jord. *Get.* 167). Their king was Geiseric, a leader of single-minded, remorseless will, a man of immense ambition and the ability to match it. As discussed previously, he was by far the cleverest of all the Germanic leaders of this period. Small wonder, therefore, Bonifatius soon found it impossible to keep his new allies within bounds, and consequently he lost much of Roman North Africa after his army, supported by a task force from the East under Aspar, went down in disastrous defeat in AD 430. Bonifatius was forced to clear out and seek the grace of Placidia in Ravenna.

There he became reconciled with Placidia, and their restored friendship inspired in her hope that he would suppress Aëtius, whom she was beginning to find excessively powerful. To the fury of Aëtius, Bonifatius was elevated to the top military command, *magister utriusque militiae*. And so the two western warlords clashed in civil war. In AD 432, at the Fifth Milestone outside Ariminum (Rimini), Bonifatius received his death wound, and a few days later died.

Following the battle, which he lost by the way, Aëtius and the remnants of his force managed to retreat to Gaul. Defeated, disgraced, declared an outlaw by Placidia, he then withdrew to a fortified estate inherited from his father, where he attempted to hold out. However, besieged by imperial troops Aëtius soon realized that his position was untenable. Accompanied by a few loyal followers, he quietly slipped away and by way of Pannonia escaped over the Danube frontier and reached the Huns, who were currently under the rule of Ruga. The king of the Huns happily granted him sanctuary (PT *ad annum* 432).

Once again, in AD 433, Aëtius retrieved his hold over the court in Ravenna with the aid of Hun auxiliaries, and for the next five or six years he employed them regularly in his campaigns. For instance, he commanded Huns during the recovery of Gaul, his main achievement being the halting of Visigoth expansion towards the Rhodanus (Rhône) in AD 436, and the merciless destruction of the Burgundian kingdom centred on Borbetomagus (Worms) the following year. Huns are not mentioned after AD 439, for their forces were to be busy elsewhere, and it is poignant to remember that in AD 451 Aëtius combined with his old Visigoth enemies in Gaul to defeat his old friend Attila at the Catalaunian Plains.

Flavius Ardabur Aspar (d. AD 471)

Upon the death of Theodosius II, who left no male heir, his elder sister Pulcheria, a woman of decisive and vigorous character, accepted as her nominal husband and as the new emperor the aged but distinguished commander Marcianus (r. AD 450–57). It was a wise choice, for he turned out to be an earnest and capable ruler who, among other things, effected important financial and administrative reforms. His advancement to the throne was due in part to the sponsorship of a man who had been his previous superior, and who began to emerge as an ominous manipulator behind the scenes. This was Flavius Aspar.

A truly remarkable man, Aspar was the extraordinarily long serving *magister utriusque militiae* of Alanic-Gothic descent who for five decades both served in and commanded the field armies of the East Roman Empire. When Theodosius sent Galla Placidia and her son Valentinianus back to Italy, the army that accompanied them was led by Ardabur and his son Aspar. During the struggle for the western throne, Ardabur was captured by Ioannes' men, but apparently he ingratiated himself with them to such an extent he was able to undermine their loyalty to the

Reverse of a gold *solidus* (Paris, Cabinet des médailles de la BNF) depicting a full-grown Valentinianus III (r. AD 425–55), minted in Ravenna at the time of his accession. He holds a long cross (Christian) in his right hand, a Nike/Archangel (victorious) in his left, and has his foot planted on a human-headed serpent (triumphant). All this of course was not true. His long reign witnessed only further dismemberment of the West. At the time of his death, virtually all of Roman North Africa, all of western Iberia and the majority of Gaul had slipped out of Roman hands. It did not leave much: just Italy itself. With him died the Theodosian house. As they say, dynasties never last.
(© Bridgeman Art Library)

usurper. With that, the rot set in and Ioannes' army became demoralized and started to disintegrate (Olymp. fr. 46). A second, less likely version of this story has the young Aspar valiantly leading his men (with the help of a messenger from God disguised as a shepherd) through the treacherous salt marshes to capture Ravenna (IA fr. 195).

Mention has already been made earlier in this work of Aspar's involvement in Roman North Africa, and when Bonifatius went home in disgrace to Italy, Aspar and the eastern forces continued the struggle against the Vandals alone. For his loyal services to the court in Ravenna he was appointed consul of the West for the year AD 434. Yet it was under Theodosius II, the eastern emperor, that Aspar was to rise to the top military command, *magister utriusque militiae*, and elevated to the rank of patrician, *patricius*. For all this, however, men of barbarian origin never really prospered in bids for the highest office in the land, though a very few did manage to steer the emperors, enigmatic men such as the half-Roman and half-Vandal Flavius Stilicho (AD 365–408). As for Aspar, we have already met him as the favourite comrade and trusted confident of the emperor Marcianus, yet greater prospects still lay ahead of him. In AD 453 Pulcheria died, ending the Theodosian house in the East. Then four years later Marcianus himself died, leaving no specific heir or designated successor. As a barbarian and an Arian Christian, Aspar could not dream of ascending the throne as emperor and starting a new dynasty, but he could play the role of kingmaker very well. Moreover, Aspar had behind him the support of a growing new Germanic element in the court at Constantinople. His choice was Leo I (r. AD 457–74), a man of obscure origin and unprepossessing qualities (Prisc. fr. 20, Candidus fr. 1).

Much to Aspar's chagrin, he soon found that Leo proved to be something different from what was expected, and in fact determined not to be merely a docile tool. His relations with Aspar soon cooled, and even became hostile (Zon. 14.1). To offset the supremacy of Aspar and his Germanic cabal at court, the emperor married his eldest daughter Ariadne to the Isaurian chief Tarasicodissa, the groom changing his name to the more acceptable Zeno. Together Leo and his henchman Zeno organized a new force of palace guards called the *excubitores*, Isaurians of Cilicia in the main and 300 strong, which gave the emperor a personal body of supporters on whom he could rely against the power of Aspar and his supporters.

Following an attempted coup d'état by his son Ardabur, which he probably knew more about than he let on and was plausibly a silent partner in this attack on the emperor, Aspar fell from grace. The same year he was liquidated during an Isaurian palace revolution, along with most of his sons and a large number of his sympathizers. With this piece of barbaric treachery the Germanic danger was abruptly removed from the court. It must have been a particularly brutal crackdown, even by the standards of the day, since the pogrom earned for Leo the rather insulting appellation 'the Butcher' (Malchus fr. 1, Candidus frs. 1, 2). It is doubtful if the incident caused him much anxiety. He had never been popular and wanted to use his authority to command obedience, not warm-heartedness.

WHEN WAR IS DONE

Despite defeat at the Catalaunian Plains, Attila was far from curbed. In the spring of the following year he invaded Italy, sacking several northern cities (Aquileia at the head of the Adriatic was destroyed) before moving southward. It seemed as if Rome would be subjected to a second and even more devastating sack. As balmy spring turned into blistering summer, however, Attila was compelled to withdraw, short of Ariminum (Rimini), only by famine and its inseparable companion, pestilence. To spoil an illusion, when Pope Leo I (AD 440–61) intervened as *pontifex ex machina* and persuaded the pagan king to turn back 'where the Mincius river is crossed at the well-travelled ford' (Jord. *Get.* 223 = Prisc. fr. 17), he probably used such non-spiritual arguments as the height of Rome's walls, the recent famine, the current plague, and the landing of an eastern army at Ravenna. He may have even paid a subsidy to Attila – Gibbon (*D&F*, chap. XXXV, p. 420) calls this payment the dowry of Honoria once demanded by Attila. He may be right.

Whatever dissuaded him, however, Attila clearly intended to invade the East Roman Empire again in AD 453 (Jord. *Get.* 225). But within a year the king was dead. He died unexpectedly during the night after marrying the latest of his innumerable wives, the Germanic princess Ildico (Prisc. fr. 23), a real beauty by all accounts. For the non-indulgent monk Jordanes, Attila's inglorious demise was a warning against the dangers of binge drinking: 'Thus did drunkenness put a disgraceful end to a famous war leader' (*Get.* 254). According to the more romantic rumours current in Roman circles he was stabbed with a knife by a woman (e.g. Mal. 14.10).

Attila's retreat from Italy had marked the ebb of the Hun's threat to the two empires. On his death, his realm was divided between his sons, who promptly squabbled his legacy to bits. Yet there is no inherent reason why a nomadic empire should not outlive its founder. It is worth remembering that a later example of this is Genghis Khan (r. AD 1206–27), who had successors as capable (and as ruthless) as himself and obviously understood

Detail of *Missorium of Aspar* (Firenze, Museo Archeologico), a large silver plate found in Cosa in 1750. Commemorating Aspar's consulship of the West in AD 434, around the rim of the plate (not shown here) an inscription (*CIL* ix 2637) reads: FL(avivs) ARDABVR ASPAR VIR INLVSTRIS COM(es) ET MAG(ister) MILITVM ET CONSVL ORDINARIIVS. In the centre of the plate (seen here) Aspar is depicted togate, seating in a *sella curulis*, holding a *mappa* and sceptre with imperial busts on it. To his left stands his eldest son, also togate and holding a *mappa*, with name and title ARDABVR IVNIOR PRETOR inscribed above him. The two men are overlooked by the personifications of Rome and Constantinople. (Sailko)

45

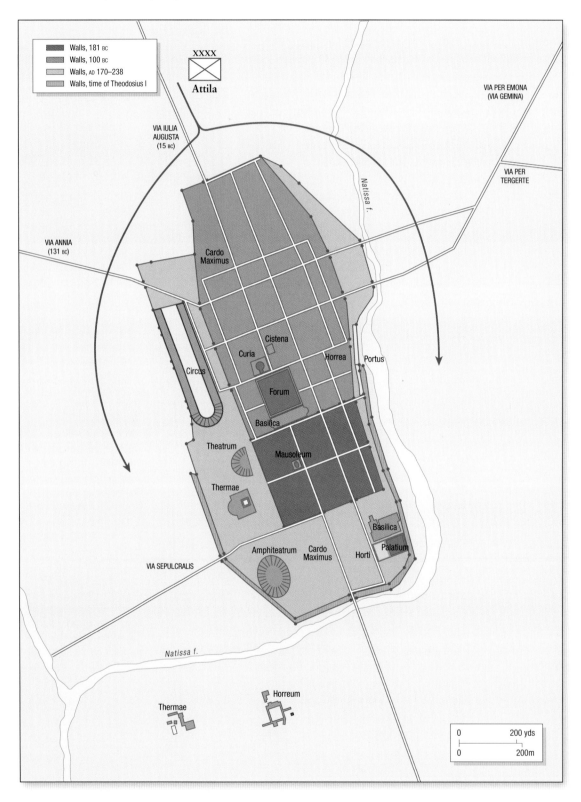

the importance of appointing an heir for securing the smooth transition of power after his death. Of course, Attila can have been under no illusion that he was going to live forever, but he still failed to secure his realm by avoiding the most common danger for a nomadic empire; the struggle over succession. Worse still, he had left behind him no true governmental machinery or institutions and deprived of his forceful personality, the Hun Empire lost its coherency and soon fell to pieces.

Inspired by Ardaric, the king of the Gepids, who had been a loyal confidant of Attila, the Ostrogoths, Heruli, Rugii, Scirii and the rest rebelled. After a succession of costly battles, the decision was reached, probably in AD 454, on the banks of the Nedao in Pannonia, an unidentified river probably somewhere in modern Slovenia. For it was here that the quarrelling sons of Attila were decisively defeated, and Ellac, the elder, killed (Jord. *Get.* 262). This crucial battle, 'far more momentous' than the Catalaunian Plains (Bury 1923: 297), ended for all times the monolithic Hun Empire, and since then it has led a purely literary existence.

The Huns themselves broke up into their various tribes, or rather into their respective clans within these tribes, and never regained the unity that had made them a serious menace to the two empires. Some would have departed into the steppes, there to renew their true nomadism, and others gravitating toward the Roman world. And so it was that in AD 469, some 15 years after the Nedao, Dengizich was killed trying to regain the former lands of his father and his head displayed publicly in Constantinople (CM *ad annum* 469). All the same, even those tribes that had returned to nomadism, such as the Onogur (or Bulgar), the Utigur and the Kotrigur Huns, continued to raid the East Roman Empire from the steppes of what is now the Ukraine. It was the latter tribe that posed the greatest threat, and Iustinianus was to endeavour to keep them from imperial lands, through various subsidies and treaties granted to them or to their neighbours.

Even so, in AD 551 a force of Kotrigurs crossed the eastern reaches of the Danubius and plundered Roman territory. Severely strapped for manpower

by this time, Iustinianus was unable to muster any of his own troops against them. Nevertheless, on this occasion he succeeded in diverting the Kotrigurs by inducing their neighbours, the Utigurs, to plunder their homeland and thus draw them back there. Since each tribe sought out its own pastures in comparative isolation, the tribal forces could act with complete independence, the one of the other. Thus, as Iustinianus appreciated, rivalry and hostility were as common among them as friendship and cooperation.

The Kotrigurs soon resumed their raids, however, and this time with vengeance. Their war chief, who bore the Iranian name Zabergan, began a vast new expedition against the East Roman Empire in late AD 558. He boldly divided his host into three bands, each with a definite sphere of operations: one assigned to Greece, one to western Thrace, and the third, under his personal command, to eastern Thrace against Constantinople itself. His audacity was justified by the circumstances of the Balkan provinces at this twilight period in Iustinianus' reign. The emperor's military resources had been squandered or exhausted in his wars of reconquest. His treasury had been drained by decades of expenditures. His fortifications were currently being used mainly as places of refuge alone, and the dilapidated Long Wall of Anastasius, which was meant to protect the hinterland of Constantinople,

'The Hun is through the gate!' – Attila razes Aquileia

For three months Attila had stood outside the great city of Aquileia. The Huns had employed a whole range of siege machines, 'a formidable train of battering rams, movable turrets, and engines, that threw stones, darts and fire' (*D&F*, chap. XXXV, p. 415). Still, Attila's machinery made little headway against the city's stout walls, and he decided on a starvation strategy.

Behind him his Hun riders waited, an impatient, dissatisfied, milling host: squat, powerfully built men with yellowish skin, slitted deep-sunk eyes, and flat beardless faces, extremely strong in the upper limbs, dressed in filthy skin garments and mounted on ugly but tough looking brutes, each man carrying a powerful asymmetrical composite bow and a densely packed quiver. His warriors were gradually losing heart. They were also lacking supplies. The prolonged siege was an unwelcome distraction for an army that relied on speed for its success and on spoils for its supplies. Attila was on the verge of retreat when an omen changed his mind. One evening he saw a stork flying out of the city carrying its young. He pointed this out, saying that the stork knew that Aquileia was about to fall to the Huns (Jord. *Get.* 219). And so it did.

In this reconstruction the Huns have broken in and are now subjecting Aquileia to a terrible fate. Attila, their king, sits patiently upon his horse. One of his men is handing him an exquisite varicoloured glass goblet, spoil from Aquileia. Till this day the city would be famed for its glass making, introduced and practised by its Judaic community, the *Orientali* or *Siriani* of Latin sources, which numbered in the thousands. That is all about to change as Aquileia has been given over to complete pillage and fire. This is what Attila is watching. His victorious Huns and Germanic allies are busy scouring the city for transportable loot, collecting prisoners, dispatching the 'useless'. Some of them are equipping themselves with Roman arms stripped from the corpses of enemy more affluent than they, and others are pillaging buildings. Aquileia is already beginning to burn. In one forgotten corner, a small band of Roman soldiers are making their 'last stand'.

The destruction inflicted on the city by Attila's army was to be total, the red hand of Hunnic war sparing neither race, age nor sex. As for that glass goblet, this will doubtless serve as a generous gift from Attila to one of his leading Huns or Germanic confederates.

was of little value. The Kotrigurs ravaged at will, bringing fire and sword to the population of Greece and Thrace. Worse of all, they were soon pasturing their nomad horses in the suburban gardens of the capital. It must have seemed that Attila himself had risen from the grave.

In this moment of humiliation and impending disaster, Iustinianus, a jealous and dangerously paranoid emperor, swallowed his pride and turned for help to another ghost of the past. Flavius Belisarius (d. AD 565) had been living in quiet retirement in Constantinople since his return from Italy in AD 548. Although the old general had long ceased active service he had lost none of his robust energy, or any of his astonishing tactical imagination. Quickly rallying to his emperor, he gathered what troops were available in the city. Most of them were worthless, though he had a core of some 300 men who were veterans of his campaigns, many of whom had remained with him as his personal body of retainers, his *bucellarii* in other words, some of whom were Huns of course.

With these pitifully limited forces, Belisarius marched out to defend the capital and what was left of Thrace. Through a masterly use of ruses and skilful positioning, he tricked Zabergan's horse warriors into thinking they were about to fall prey to a great army. They abandoned their attack on Constantinople and withdrew from Thrace (Agath. 5.14.6–20.8). Elsewhere the Kotrigurs' advance was finally stalled, and engorged with their booty they sluggishly straggled homeward. Iustinianus was in no position to strike the raiders on their way out of imperial territory, but he was able once again through diplomatic means to incite the Utigurs against the Kotrigurs (Agath. 5.25, Men. fr. 2). The two tribes thereafter wasted themselves in internecine conflict until the Turkic Avars, on becoming the new major power in the Danube basin, absorbed them.

In the words of one modern scholar, when a confederacy disintegrates and

Aerial view of the seaport of Ravenna. In our period of study the easily defended city of Ravenna was now the capital of the West. In AD 401/2 the site of the old Augustan eastern fleet, the *classis Ravennas*, had been selected as such by Honorius not because it was nearer to the danger zone but because it was practically inaccessible to invaders by land, being almost surrounded by stretches of water and salt marsh. (Marek Śluysarczyk)

disappears, 'the camps, the clans, and in part the tribes also, retain an organic life' (Peisker *apud* Thompson 1948: 182). Indeed, Peisker even speaks of the 'indestructibility' of the camps and the clans, and by this line of reasoning therefore Attila's great empire was little more than a short-lived robber state. The courts of the two empires alike may have felt themselves freed from the frightful threat that Attila had represented in his lifetime, but in his lifetime Attila was only building up his vested interest in a particular kind of power of limited range. Whereas he could pursue external expansion, he could not aim at wide conquest. The natural direction for the latter was the two empires, but this would have meant reaching out for a new kind of power, without staking his valuable vested interest on the ability to master the two courts and to hold off potential rivals from within his empire while doing so – Attila's secretaries kept a list of those of them who were being sheltered by the Romans (Prisc. fr. 8). The fall of his sons after his death shows how difficult this was. The truth is the natural instinct to defend what he already had limited the scope of Attila's political outlook and activity. He never made that transformation from a successful war chief to world conqueror.

Panoramic view of Udine from the Castello di Udine, looking north-west to north-east towards the distant Julian Alps. Hungarian legend has it that Attila built the castle hill when he was besieging nearby Aquileia. As the local landscape was completely flat, he instructed his men to bring soil in their helmets, the resulting artificial mound being crowned with a square tower. Actually, the hill itself is composed of the detritus that has accumulated over the centuries, while the earliest reference to any type of building on top of it dates to AD 983 and refers to a *castrum*. (Robert Mucchiutti)

INSIDE THE MIND

'A subtle man who fought with artifice before he waged his wars', so wrote Jordanes (*Get.* 186) describing the king of the Huns. Jordanes arrived at this aphoristic analysis of Attila's psyche probably through reading his well-thumbed copy of Priscus' *History*. I shall have something to say later about the significance of this fragmentary work.

Since peace was cheaper than war and ambassadors cheaper than armies, the eastern emperor Theodosius II sent a diplomatic mission to the subtle Attila. Yet these ambassadors, the erudite Priscus amongst their number, who tried to negotiate with the king, found him saturnine, sallow, capricious and contemplative, but as he was confronted with treachery on all sides this moodiness is hardly surprising. There was at least one assassination attempt against him that we know of, probably others that we will never know of. After all, Attila was the ruler of a people known for violence towards and from their rulers, and as such, he would have had to deal with all manner of enemies, all manner of friends, and all those in between. A powerful enemy abroad is not so much to be feared as dissension in your own camp.

Yet the dreadful portrait of Attila was not simply one of repression and tyranny. For the Roman ambassadors would have also noted that even when gold and gems were freely available the king himself still wore simple clothes, ate off wooden plates and never tasted the luxury of bread. His throne too was simple, being no more than a wooden seat (Prisc. fr. 8). Perhaps, like Genghis Khan after him, it was covered with a black felted wool rug to remind him of his origins. During his residence at the seat of empire, the king of the Huns, unlike a Roman emperor, could maintain his superior dignity without concealing his person from the public view, which he did without the slightest pomp, panoply or parade. There was nothing superfluous about Attila in the way of flesh, neither was there anything about his rulership that could be regarded as superfluous, in method nor manner. His world was faces, not bowed heads. Ostentation he obviously abhorred, and the most Attila claimed for himself was that he was 'of noble birth, having succeeded his father Mundiuch, and he has preserved his high descent' (Prisc. fr. 12).

Retaining much of the simplicity and vigour of the genuine steppe nomad – though he was probably born somewhere on the *puszta* – Attila's greatest crime was to be different, in physical appearance, cultural background and attitude towards urban civilization. Naturally, his foes raised him to the status of a demon, the avatar of desolation and destruction. Yet his greatest memorial is his role as the wise Etzel in the complex medieval German epic poem *Nibelungenlied*, which inspired Wagner's rather overblown operatic cycle of *Der Ring des Nibelungen*. Doing what a bard worth his salt would do, Wagner cherry picked what best suited him from Germanic and Norse

West face of Proconnesian marble plinth supporting the Obelisk of Karnak, Hippodrome, Istanbul. Enthroned in the imperial box, Theodosius I, the last ruler of a united Roman Empire, flanked by the adolescent cypher Valentinianus II (his left), and his sons, Arcadius and Honorius (his right), is receiving tribute from the kneeling chieftains of vanquished Goths. It was this striking image of imperial power that Attila was to turn upside down. (Gryffindor)

legends, opting mainly for Norse mythology – a hoard of gold, a ring of power, a helmet of invisibility, gods, giants, a fire breathing dragon, magical warrior maidens – rejected history, and dropped the courteous and civilized Etzel completely.

Whether or not the real Attila was courteous and civilized is neither here nor there, but Priscus suggests a more positive and complex picture of the Hun king than just an accursed enemy. He was a ruthless warlord, to be sure. But in other respects it was possible he could be both wise and tolerant. He seemed to be a loving father, at least to one of his sons, and allowed his principal wife Herekan to have a position of authority. He was certainly capable of clemency, for he pardoned the would-be assassin hired by Theodosius' chief eunuch, Chrysaphius. This courtier permitted ethics to play little part in his diplomacy, and assassination was a perfectly legitimate method to dispose of an enemy. This is not to say that Attila was a paragon of patrician virtue, far from it, but we have no evidence that he acted in a similar manner. His clemency, nevertheless, was always tempered by a resolve to act forcefully, if need be savagely. He could impale, he could crucify.

In any circumstances, Attila's first consideration was always the protection of his own rule. Many pastoral peoples worshipped, venerated or swore by their swords, sometimes seeing in one particular weapon a mystic symbol of divine support. Before the Huns, the Scythians and the Xiongnu both had their sword cults, so did the Avars after them. According to Herodotos, the Scythians 'set up an ancient iron sword, which serves as an idol representing Ares' (4.62.2), over which they pour the blood of

South face of the aforesaid plinth, showing Germanic *scholares* (Goths in the East, Franks in the West) of the *scholae palatinae* protecting Theodosius (centre), Valentinianus (his left), and Arcadius and Honorius (his right). Like most Germanic warriors of the time, they wear their hair long, adorn themselves with *torques*, and are armed with large oval shields and long spears. As titular lord of the West, Honorius would employ large numbers of Huns as well as Goths and Franks, while his half-sister Galla Placidia retained a private army of Visigoth *bucellarii*. (Georges Jusoone)

prisoners of war. It is recorded that at the conclusion of a treaty of alliance between the Xiongnu and the Han dynasty:

> (Han) Chang and (Chang) Meng, together with the *shan-yü* [khan of a tribal confederation] and the elders went up the Mountain of the Xiongnu by the east side of the river No-shui, and impaled a white horse. The *shan-yü* took a costly sword and moistened its tip with wine; they drank the dedicated wine from the skull of a Yue-chi lord who had been killed by the *shan-yü* Laoshan. (Sima Qian *Shiji* 92)

The drinking of sacred wine from the skull of a detested foe thereby sealed the negotiations between the Chinese envoys and the *shan-yü*.

The Huns also possessed a sword cult. Their shamanist beliefs and customs were deep-rooted, and shortly after Attila came to power he made the cult his own. Priscus, later to be quoted by Jordanes, heard the original story. It seems that one particular sword – Latinized as the sword of Mars – had always been esteemed by the Huns, but had been lost. However, a herdsman noticed one day that one of his cattle was lame and that its foot had been cut. Following the trail of blood to its source, the herdsman found an ancient sword buried in the grass. He pulled it up and brought it to Attila, who 'rejoiced at this gift and being of great courage he decided he had been appointed to be the ruler of the whole world and that, thanks to the sword of Mars, he had been granted the power to win wars' (Jord. *Get.* 183 = Prisc. fr. 10). It seems Attila based his supremacy on the solid foundations of his peoples' ancient superstitions, his followers believing

Frankish arms (Nuremberg, Germanisches Nuremberg Nationalmuseum) from warrior burials. Frankish helmets – this one is a *spangenhelm* – are rare finds and presumably were rarely worn except by the most socially elevated. The *francisca* was the most distinctive axe of the period, the leitmotif that Isidorus Hispalensis (*Etymologiae* 18.6.9) supposed had given the Franks their name. It was single bladed with a heavy metal head weighting around 11kg, and could be hurled with great accuracy just before contact with the foe, often with devastating effect. We see also a double-edged sword, a single-bladed *scramasaxe* (OE *seax*), and a cone-shaped shield-boss. Franks fought for both sides at the Catalaunian Plains. (Altaipanther)

54

his authority derived from the sword of Mars itself. Of course there was also his force of personality, and anyone who questioned his right to rule would have to fight not only Attila, but the divine powers as well. The sword was to be taken as a sign that his right to rule was divine. His rise to power was no accident of fate; on the contrary, it was part of a divinely ordained plan. There is a strong possibility that his zeal was a political device to consolidate his rule and strengthen his legitimacy. If so, it was an astute one.

Alongside his undoubted skill as a leader of his people and his claim to the divine favour of the war god, it was Attila's lavish reward of loyal comrades and confederates that helped guarantee his own continued dominance. He thereby gained a reputation for generosity, a highly regarded trait in nomadic society. In return he demanded full devotion and obedience, and whoever failed in this was harshly punished. His generosity was obviously a powerful and well-oiled weapon. But this was not the whole of it. Part of the mystique of Attila's leadership was his self-confidence, part his personal austerity, and of course part his generosity in friendship. He could be made a firm friend, but no mercy could be expected from him as an enemy. Truly, to his enemies Attila was not only merciless, but cruel and brutal too. Here was a man who was in full control of his world, or if not, was quite ready to do what was required to bring it under control.

Attila kept his followers because he could reward them handsomely. In the world of pastoralism on the steppes, 'a generous lord had many followers, a weak or unsuccessful one soon had none' (Fox 1936: 49). Before taking this further we must digress and consider the fate of Uldin. Sometime in late AD 408 Uldin, the first Hun leader whom we know by name, crossed the Danubius and raided deep into Thrace. Though a very rugged and fragmented landscape, the broad plains of Thrace were productive and relatively densely settled. When the Romans tried to buy him off, he rejected their offer: when the Roman envoy made this proposal to him, Uldin merely pointed towards the rising sun and said that, if he so wished, he would find it easy to subdue all the lands on which the sun shone. He demanded an impossible sum as the price of peace, but the envoy was not at a loss. He protracted the negotiations with Uldin and at the same time entered into secret talks with his senior officers. His propositions (and payoffs) were agreeable. Many of Uldin's followers deserted, and he himself only escaped with difficulty. Many of those who decided to stay with him on his desperate dash to the Danubius were captured and carted off to Constantinople in chains (Soz. 9.5.2–7, cf. *CTh.* v.6.2, 3).

The rise and fall of Uldin reflects the fragile position of Hun leaders. In early AD 401 he had dealt directly with the eastern emperor Arcadius, and in AD 406 had taken his followers west to serve as mercenaries under the western generalissimo Stilicho, helping to defeat the Goths of Radagaesus at Faesulae (*Chron. Min.* 1.65251, Zos. 5.22.3, 26.4, Oros. 7.37.16, CM *ad annum* 406). It can be said, therefore, that a Hunnic warlord had continually to rouse himself to keep his followers well supplied and to present them with a good share of the booty and the costliest gifts.

A LIFE IN WORDS

Excursus was a favourite device of Graeco-Roman authors, wishing to expand on a topic not necessarily connected with the narrative. A famous example is of course Ammianus Marcellinus' 'Excursus on the Huns' in his *Res Gestae*, which also happens to be the only surviving account of the Huns before Attila. The author, when he first turns to describe the Huns, at once speaks of their loathsome personal appearance. He can find no words strong enough to express his horror of the new barbarians (AM 31.2.2). His prejudice was soon to be taken up by Claudian (*In Ruf.* 1.325), who in turn was followed by Priscus (fr. 10), Sidonius Apollinaris (*Carm.* 2.245), Procopius (*Wars* 1.3.4–5) and Jordanes (*Get.* 127–28). It is Jerome (d. AD 419), Christian scholar and future saint, who neatly summarizes this prejudice up when he says, 'the soldiers of Rome … tremble and shrink in fear at the sight of them' (*Ep.* 60.17). It sounds as if the Huns simply terrified their way into victory.

The hideous facial appearance and tattered skin garments of these horse-borne invaders may have utterly unnerved the soldiers of the two empires, but it is a well-known fact that the further removed in physical appearance, language and culture an ethnic group is, the more they are distrusted. This is why the contemporary late antique writers viewed the Huns as grotesque and sinister, deceitful and fickle, hot tempered and burning with greed – vile creatures of an exceedingly disagreeable kind. When they first attracted the

Copy of the *Missorium of Theodosius* (Mérida, Museo Nacional de Arte Romano), a ceremonial silver dish made for the *decennalia* in AD 388 of Theodosius I (r. AD 378–95). In hierarchical pose, he is flanked by Valentinianus II (his right) and his eldest son Arcadius (his left). The *scholae palatinae*, identified by their hairstyles, *torques*, spears and shields, are Germanic (Goths in the East, Franks in the West). By the mid-5th century AD the West had become a cocktail of cultures; consequently there seem to have been no real 'Roman' soldiers left, only Germanic mercenaries or allied *foederati*. Thus, at the Catalaunian Plains we would be very hard pressed to distinguish between a 'Roman' soldier (perhaps born a Visigoth) serving in the army of Aëtius and a 'Visigoth' warrior (perhaps born a Roman) in that of Theodoric. (Manuel Parada López de Corselas)

attention of Ammianus Marcellinus in the last quarter of the 4th century AD, Hun auxiliaries (*Chunis auxiliantibus*) were playing a large and helpful part in the armies of Theodosius I (*Pan. lat.* ii (xii) 32.4, IA fr. 187). No matter to our author, for the Huns still appear to him as scarcely human:

> You cannot make a truce with them, because they are quite unreliable and easily swayed by any breath of rumour that promises an advantage; like unreasoning beasts they are entirely at the mercy of the maddest impulses. They are totally ignorant of the distinction between right and wrong, their speech is shifty and obscure, and they are under no restraint from religion or superstition. Their greed for gold is prodigious, and they are so fickle and prone to anger that often in a single day they will quarrel with their allies without provocation, and then make it up again without anyone attempting to reconcile them. (AM 31.2.11)

Ammianus Marcellinus gives the Hun the outlook of a wolf; it delights in cruelty, is keen to make gains and knows nothing of good faith, ritual, or virtuous behaviour. The accuracy of his statements is of less interest than the fact they were made close to the time and the author was more than likely stating what his narrow circle of well-educated, well-to-do readers wanted to hear, happy to be swept along by the author's exaggerations. Thus, despite being an excellent authority, this particular piece appears to be an example of vilification on the author's part, all the long-standing

The Great Wall of China at Jinshinling, Hebai province. During the period of the Warring States, several states had built walls of rammed earth to protect their frontiers: the Qin dynasty (221–206 BC) linked three of these to form the beginnings of the Great Wall, beyond which the security of China gave way to the vast and inhospitable steppe over which the Xiongnu roamed. The wall governed movement and trade between China and the north, and was a military barrier too, but only against low-level raids. (Severin.stalder)

classical prejudices and well-worn literary stereotypes coming out all over again. Whether or not he had ever seen a Hun in the flesh is naturally quite irrelevant to our author. The first seeds of Hunnophobia had been sown, and its fruit would prove to be remarkably durable.

We can only wonder at what Ammianus Marcellinus would have made and said of the greatest Hun of all, Attila. Priscus of Panium, on the other hand, was a commentator who had first-hand experience of the European Huns when Attila held the *puszta*. As we all know, our noted scholar had served on the Roman mission sent by Theodosius II to the court of the Hunnic king in the early summer of AD 449. Indeed, it is fortunate that Priscus devoted a quite disproportionate amount of his *History*, which covers the period from AD 433 to 474, to a narrative of what he saw and did in the court of Attila. He wrote in Greek and as a historian was clearly influenced by the great Attic descriptive writers, Herodotos and Xenophon. He was also, like Thucydides, a reporter of current events in which he participated. Writing for an elite audience, he was concerned with literary effect as much as accuracy, and thus lacks a flair for the details of military matters and geography. Even so, there is no doubt that he travelled with his wits about him and his eyes open. For we are indebted to him for an unforgettable *tableau vivant* of Attila the man, his wooden palace and polyglot court, the etiquette of the royal repast, and an almost unbelievably detailed account of his own journeying in territories then under Hun control, in which curiosity often extends to admiration. Is the *History* a good source? It is the only one we have. Priscus published this work, eight books originally of which only fragments remain as excerpts, soon after AD 476.

Despite Priscus, however, for the majority of Europeans Attila the Hun looms large as a deplorable character, one who has left a pall of terror over European history, the biggest and greatest calamity of his time. He left no legacy beyond disorder and destruction. After his death, the sprawling tribal conglomerate he had created was wiped from the slate of history, leaving no mark on posterity except an entirely negative memory of massacre and mayhem with which the name of Attila will ever be associated. Few of us would have liked to live under Attila's rule, yet in retrospect he was no proto-Tamerlane, whose imperial progress was marked with heaps of skulls. To dismiss Attila as the sum of all evil is to completely misunderstand a historical picture that is infinitely more complex than notions of good guy and bad guy, of war and peace. It was a very different world and a very different mind-set.

In Roman eyes of course, Priscus' acute observations notwithstanding, Attila was essentially the vulgar and unlettered leader of a shepherd people, a savage, barbarian tyrant. Yet nothing suggests to us moderns that in the vast landscape of his ambition he had a grand design with regards to world conquest. An illiterate military genius named Temüjin, formerly the unknown son of a minor Mongolian chieftain, whose fame was destined to eclipse even that of Alexander the Great, had a dream to conquer the earth. Genghis Khan, as he was to become known, and his equally restless and ambitious successors almost achieved this. Attila, however, was not a proto-Genghis. Nonetheless, the Hun king did have the vision, the strength of purpose, and the will to learn, to make the one dream he did have succeed, namely the forging of his people into a great nation, an empire of the vast Eurasian steppes bridging the rich realms of Rome and China.

Attila, in the words of Jordanes, 'alone united the realms of Scythia and Germania' (*Get.* 257, cf. 178). 'Scythia' was an imprecise term, implying roughly the whole of the Eurasian steppe region, and indeed 'Scythians' was the same generic label that Herodotos had used almost 1,000 years earlier. In our period of study the late antique sources habitually give 'new' peoples old names, with that Huns and Goths are called 'Scythians'. Philostorgius, for example, calls the Visigoths the 'greatest and most excellent of all the Scythian peoples' (11.8), while Priscus employs the term 'Scythian' as a generic term for all northern nomads, including the Huns, who are a specific race.

When the Huns first crossed into Europe out of the east they were illiterate. When they finally vanished in the turmoil of the 7th century AD, they were still illiterate. Apart from the archaeological evidence from the middle Danube region, we have to rely almost exclusively on what we are told by late antique chroniclers for the story of the Huns. Due to their perceptions of their impact upon the two empires, contemporary writers wrote of the Huns with fear and loathing, characterizing their culture as crude, and their behaviour as bestial. They were succeeded by Christian chroniclers, who condemned the Huns as devilish pagans and regarded them as an instrument sent by God to punish people for their sins. Civilizations are articulate, though the records are loaded against peoples who cannot answer back.

BIBLIOGRAPHY

Alföldi, A., 1932. 'Funde aus der Hunnenzeit und ihre ethnische Sonderung'. *Acta Archaeologia Hungarica* 9

Bäuml, F. & Birnbaum, M., 1993. *Attila: The Man and His Image*. Budapest: Corvina

Bergman, C. A., McEwen, E. & Miller, R., 1988. 'Experimental archery: projectile velocities and comparison of bow performances'. *Antiquity* 62: 658–70

Bóna, I., 1992. *Das Hunnenreich*. Budapest: Corvina

Biran, M., 2007. *Chinggis Khan*. Oxford: Oneworld Publications

Bury, J. B., 1923 (2nd edn.). *History of the Later Roman Empire*. London: Macmillan

——, 1928. *The Invasion of Europe by the Barbarians*. London: Macmillan

Di Cosmo, N. (ed.), 2001. *Warfare in Inner Asian History (500–1800)*. Leiden: E. J. Brill (Handbook of Oriental Studies 6)

——, 2002, 2004. *Ancient China and its Enemies: The Rise of Nomadic Power in East Asian History*. Cambridge: Cambridge University Press

Elton, H., 1996, 1997. *Warfare in Roman Europe, AD 350–425*. Oxford: Clarendon Press

Fields, N., 2006. *The Hun: Scourge of God, AD 375–565*. Oxford: Osprey (Warrior 111)

Fox, R. W., 1936. *Genghis Khan*. London: John Lane

Freeman, E. A., 1887. 'Aetius and Boniface'. *English Historical Review* 2.7: 417–65

Gibbon, E. (ed. & abr. D. Womersley), 2000. *The History of the Decline and Fall of the Roman Empire*. London: Penguin Books

Goffart, W., 1980. *Barbarians and Romans, AD 418–584*. Princeton, NJ: Princeton University Press

Goffart, W., 2008. 'Rome's final conquest: the Barbarians'. *History Compass* 6: 1–29

Gordon, C. D., 2013 (rev. edn.). *The Age of Attila*. Ann Arbor, MI: University of Michigan Press

Grant, M., 1990 (rev. edn.). *The Fall of the Roman Empire*. New York: Macmillan Publishing

Greer, J. P., 1975. *The Armies and Enemies of Ancient China*. Worthing: Wargames Research Group

Grousset, R. (trans. N. Walford), 1970. *The Empire of the Steppe: A History of Central Asia*. New Brunswick, NJ: Rutgers University Press

Harris, J., 1994. *Sidonius Apollinaris and the Fall of Rome, AD 407–485*. Oxford: Oxford University Press

Heather, P., 1991. *Goths and Romans*. Oxford: Oxford University Press

——, 2006. *The Fall of the Roman Empire: A New History of Rome and the Barbarians*. Oxford: Oxford University Press

Hodgkin, T., 1892 (2nd edn.). *Italy and her Invaders*. Oxford: Clarendon Press

——, 1996. *Huns, Vandals, and the Fall of the Roman Empire*. Mechanicsburg, PA: Stackpole Books

Holum, K., 1982. *Theodosian Empresses: Women and Imperial Dominion in Late Antiquity*. Los Angeles/Berkeley: University of California Press

Howarth, P., 1994, 1997. *Attila, King of the Huns: The Man and the Myth*. London: Constable

Hyun Jin Kim, 2013. *The Huns, Rome and the Birth of Europe*. Cambridge: Cambridge University Press

Jones, A. H. M., 1964. *The Later Roman Empire, AD 284–602*. Oxford: Oxford University Press

Karasulas, A., 2004. *Mounted Archers of the Steppe, 600 BC–AD 1300*. Oxford: Osprey (Elite 120)

Kassai, L., 2002. *Horseback Archery*. Budapest: Püski Kiadó

Kelly, C., 2008. *Attila the Hun: Barbarian Terror and the Fall of the Roman Empire*. London: Bodley Head

Laing, J., 2000. *Warriors of the Dark Age*. Stroud: Sutton

Lattimore, O., 1940. *Inner Asian Frontiers of China*. New York: American Geographical Society (Research Series no. 21)

Liebeschuetz, J. H. W. G., 1991. *Barbarians and Bishops*. Oxford: Clarendon Press

Lindner, R. P., 1981. 'Nomadism, horses and Huns'. *Past & Present* 92: 1–19

MacGeorge, P., 2002. *Late Roman Warlords*. Oxford: Oxford University Press

Maenchen-Helfen, O. J., 1944–45. 'Huns and Hsiung-nu'. *Byzantion* 17: 222–43

——, 1944–45. 'The legends of the origins of the Huns'. *Byzantion* 17: 244–51

——, 1973. *The World of the Huns*. Los Angeles/Berkeley: University of California Press

Man, J., 2004. *Genghis Khan: Life, death and Resurrection*. London: Bantam Press

——, 2005. *Attila: The Barbarian King who Challenged Rome*. London: Bantam Press

Massey, D., 1994. 'Roman archery tested'. *Military Illustrated* 74: 36–39

McEwen, E., 1978. 'Nomadic archery: some observations on composite bow design and construction', in P. Denwood (ed.), *Arts of the Eurasian Steppelands*. London: School of Oriental and African Studies, 188–202

McLeod, W. E., 1965. 'The range of the ancient bow'. *Phoenix* 19: 1–14

Merrills, A., & Miles, R., 2010. *The Vandals*. Oxford: Oxford University Press

Mommsen, T., 1901. 'Aëtius'. *Hermes* 36: 516–47

Moss, J. R., 1973. 'The effects of the policies of Aëtius on the history of western Europe'. *Historia* 72: 711–31

Nicolle, D., 1990. *Attila and the Nomad Hordes*. Oxford: Osprey (Elite 30)

——, 1995, 1999. *Medieval Warfare Source Book: Warfare in Western Christendom*. London: Brockhampton Press

O'Donnell, J. J., 2008, 2009. *The Ruin of the Roman Empire: A New History*. London: Profile Books

Oost, S. I., 1968. *Galla Placidia Augusta*. Chicago: University of Chicago Press

Rudenko, S. I. (trans. H. Pollems), 1969. *Die Kultur der Hsiung-Nu und die Hügelgräber von Noin Ula*. Bonn: Rudolf Habelt

—— (trans. M. W. Thompson), 1970. *Frozen Tombs of Siberia: The Pazyryk Burials of Iron-age Horsemen*. London: J. M. Dent & Sons

Selby, S., 2000, 2003. *Chinese Archery*. Hong Kong: Hong Kong University Press

Sinor, D., 1972. 'Horse and pasture in Inner Asian history'. *Oriens extremis* 19: 171–83

—— (ed.), 1987. *History of Early Inner Asia*. Cambridge University Press

Täeckholm, U., 1969. 'Aëtius and the battle on the Catalaunian Fields'. *Opuscula Romana* 7: 259–76

Thompson, E. A., 1945. 'The Camp of Attila'. *Journal of Hellenic Studies* 65: 112–15

——, 1948. *A History of Attila and the Huns*. Oxford: Clarendon Press

——, 1982. *Romans and Barbarians: The Decline of the Western Empire*. Madison, WI: University of Wisconsin Press

Vainshtein, S. (trans. M. Colenso), 1980. *Nomads of South Siberia: The Pastoral Economies of Tuva*. Cambridge: Cambridge University Press (Cambridge Studies in Social Anthropology 25)

Vaissière, E., de la, 2005. 'Huns et Xiongnu'. *Central Asiatic Journal* 49: 3–26

Wolfram, H. (trans. T. J. Dunlap), 1988. *History of the Goths*. Los Angeles/Berkeley: University of California Press

——, 1997. *The Roman Empire and Its Germanic Peoples*. Los Angeles/Berkeley: University of California Press

Wijnendaele, J., 2014. *The Last of the Romans: Bonifatius – Warlord and Comes Africae, 413–433 AD*. London: Bloomsbury Publishing

ABBREVIATIONS

Agath.	Agathias Scholasticus, *Histories*
AM	Ammianus Marcellinus, *Res Gestae*
CM	Count Marcellinus, *Chronica*
Cass. *Var.*	Cassiodorus, *Variae*
Chron. Min.	*Chronica Minora*
CIL	T. Mommsen et al., *Corpus Inscriptionum Latinarum* (Berlin, 1862 onwards)
Claud. *In Ruf.*	Claudian, *In Rufinum*
CTh.	T. Mommsen et al., *Codex Theodosianus* (Berlin, 1904)
D&F	E. Gibbon, *The History of the Decline and Fall of the Roman Empire*
Ep.	Jerome, *Epistulae*
Epit.	Vegetius, *Epitoma rei militaris*
GT	Gregory of Tours, *Historia Francorum*
HV	Isidorus, *Historia de regibus Gothorum, Vandalorum et Suevorum*
IA	Ioannes Antiochensis (Gordon trans.)
ILS	H. Dessau, *Inscriptiones Latinae Selectae* (Berlin, 1892–1916)
Jord. *Get.*	Jordanes, *Getica = de origine actibusque Getarum*
Mal.	Malalas, *Chronographia*
Men.	Menander Protector, *Histories*
Mul.	Vegetius, *Digesta Artis Mulomedicinae*
Olymp.	Olympiodoros (Gordon trans.)
Oros.	Orosius, *Historiae adversus Paganos*
Pan. lat.	*Panegyrici latini*
Philo.	Philostorgius, *Historia ecclesiastica*
Prisc.	Priscus, *History* (Gordon trans.)
PT	Prosper Tiro of Aquitaine, *Chronica*
SA *Carm.*	Sidonius Apollinaris, *Carmina*
SA *Ep.*	Sidonius Apollinaris, *Epistulae*
SA *PA*	Sidonius Apollinaris, *Panegyric on Avitus*
Soz.	Sozomen, *Historia ecclesiastica*
Wars	Procopius, *Wars*
Zon.	Zonaras, *Epitome historiarum*
Zos.	Zosimus, *Historia nova*

GLOSSARY

Aventail – ring mail attached to rim of helmet to protect the neck

Bucellarii 'hardtack-eaters' – armed retainers of Roman commander

Bucellatum 'hardtack' – double-baked campaign bread

Comes/comites 'companion' – translated as count, commander of a field force

Comes domesticorum – commander of the *domestici* protecting emperor

Comitatus/comitatensis – field army

Dux/duces 'leader' – translated as duke, commander of sector of frontier

Excubitores 'those out of bed' – 300-strong crack fighting unit protecting eastern Roman emperor

Fabrica/fabricae – state-run armaments factory

Foederati – barbarian soldiers, under their ethnic leaders, serving Roman emperor

Koumiss – mildly fermented mare's milk

Lames/lamellae – narrow vertical plate

Leuva – Gaulish distance approximating to 1.5 Roman miles (1,500 Roman paces = 2.22km)

Magister equitum – Master of Cavalry

Magister utriusque militiae – Master of Both Services or simply Master of Soldiers

Magister officiorum – Master of Offices

Magister peditum – Master of Infantry

Mappa – napkin indicating senatorial/patrician rank

Mille passus/milia passuum 'one-thousand paces' – Roman mile = 1.48km

Praesentalis 'in the presence' – title given to senior Roman commander attending the emperor himself

Pteruges 'feathers' – leather fringing on armour

Scholae palatinae 'Palatine Schools' – household troops protecting Roman emperor under Master of Offices

Solidus/solidi – late Roman gold coin (4.54g/0.22oz. = 5/6th weight of the old *aureus*, 72 *solidi* = 1 Roman pound)

Spangenhelm – segmented and framed conical helmet of Danubian origin

Torque – neck ornament worn by Roman elite soldiers or military commanders

INDEX

References to illustrations are shown in **bold**.